Twayne's United States Authors Series

EDITOR OF THIS VOLUME

Warren French

Indiana University

W. S. Merwin

TUSAS 360

W. S. Merwin

W. S. MERWIN

By CHERI DAVIS

University of Leicester
Leicester, England

TWAYNE PUBLISHERS
A DIVISION OF G. K. HALL & CO., BOSTON

Copyright © 1981 by G. K. Hall & Co.

Published in 1981 by Twayne Publishers,
A Division of G. K. Hall & Co.
All Rights Reserved

Printed on permanent/durable acid-free paper and bound in the
United States of America

First Printing

Frontispiece photo © Thomas Victor, 1979, to be used only in
conjunction with Twayne USA hardcover first edition of this book.

Library of Congress Cataloging in Publication Data

Davis, Cheri, 1944–
W. S. Merwin.

(Twayne's United States authors series ; TUSAS 360)
Bibliography: p. 171–75
Includes index.
1. Merwin, William S., 1927–   —Criticism and interpretation.
PS3563.E75Z64   818'.54'09   80-26134
ISBN 0-8057-7301-0

For
Mary and Edward Colby
and Tim Langdell

Contents

About the Author

Cheri Colby Davis was born in Santa Monica, California. Raised in California, Indiana, and Hawaii, she attended Vassar College for two years, majoring in English. She then worked for a year at M.I.T. Press in Cambridge, Massachusetts. After spending a summer in Grenoble, France, and studying French at Boston University during her junior year, she returned to Europe in the summer of 1966, this time to Wurzburg, Germany, there to master the rudiments of the German language. And after graduating from Boston University with a B.A. in Romance Languages and Literatures (French), she pursued graduate studies in Comparative Literature at the University of Southern California. There she first attended a poetry reading given by W. S. Merwin. As an N.D.E.A. (Title IV) Fellow in Comparative Literature at the University of Southern California, she continued to pursue her studies of French and German literature. After earning a Master's degree in 1969, she specialized in French Symbolist poetry. Later, however, she focused on the continuity of American poetry and its rapport with the French Symbolists. From 1970 on, she did research on W. S. Merwin, completing her doctoral dissertation in 1973. The current study evolved naturally from her dissertation, which was entitled "Radical Innocence: A Thematic Study of the Relationship between the Translator and the Translated in the Poetry of W. S. Merwin and Jean Follain."

Having finished her work at the University of Southern California, she moved to Fallbrook, in San Diego County, and took a job in the Division of Comparative World Studies at United States International University, San Diego. The following year, 1974–75, she spent at the University of California, Riverside, as a Visiting Assistant Professor of English. There she helped design a double major in Law and Society and taught American literature, publishing two articles on W. S. Merwin.

From 1975 to 1979, she taught in the English Department of California State University, Chico. She maintains an irregular correspondence with W. S. Merwin and has published articles on his poetry and translations in *Modern Poetry Studies*, *Concerning Poetry*, and *Phantasm*. Her review of the collected works of Alain Chartier appeared in

Romanic Review. She writes and translates poetry, and upon completion of this book will devote more time to reviewing books of poetry for *Quarterly West* and *Small Press Review*.

At present she is writing a book on women and literature, and she lives with her husband Tim Langdell in London.

Preface

The achievement of W. S. Merwin is acclaimed as one of the most respected and impressive of all the poets writing in America today. Winner of the Pulitzer Prize in 1971 and recipient of a score of other major poetry prizes, grants, and fellowships, Merwin is at the vanguard in contemporary poetry and translation. He displays a virtuoso's agility in adopting a diversity of poetic forms and styles. He writes parables and psalms, chants and aphorisms, surrealistic monologues and haiku. All who read Merwin remark on the variety in his work; my goal is to reveal its underlying unity.

As I am primarily concerned with clarifying the nature and value of Merwin's writing, biography and literary history are firmly subordinated to a consideration of the poems, prose, and translations themselves. My aim has been to build a solid foundation on which a reader of Merwin's poetry might base an understanding of his work. I dwell on his attitudes toward language and silence, the centrality of animals and ecology in his work, and his beliefs about poetry and nothingness. Many of the statements I make about Merwin come from ideas generated in personal conversation with him.

A Prologue to the first chapter places Merwin in context of contemporary American poets and poetic schools. Then a brief biographical introduction is followed by a treatment of his first two books of poetry. The succeeding books of poetry are treated in Chapters 2 through 5, and Chapter 6 focuses on the two volumes of prose. Chapter 7 provides a summary and conclusion. As a new book of Merwin's translations is due soon, I regret that both this book's scope and spatial constraints forbade a fuller treatment of the translations. Although technically speaking, the translations are outside Merwin's corpus, they extend his sensibility and range and enable him to try out other voices and poetic forms. In analyzing the poems, prose, and translations, I take into account the overall evolution of Merwin's work, imagery, and thought.

Because of the limitations on space, I have had to leave many a colorful byway unexplored—the thematic parallels between Dante, T. S. Eliot, and Merwin in *A Mask for Janus* and *The Dancing Bears,* for instance. By the same token, some critics of Merwin's work—Robert Peters and Vern Rutsala among them—are unrepresented here. Still,

I hope the book serves as a consortium for the major critics of Merwin's poetry and provides insight into the continuity of his work: my intention has been to make the poetry and prose accessible to the reader who is beginning his study of Merwin here.

I wish to acknowledge the friendly support of Marshall Van Deusen, Bruce Kawin, John Ganim, and Edwin Eigner, without whose guidance and enthusiasm the book might never have been launched. I am also indebted to Gary Thompson and George Keithley for their constructive criticism of the manuscript. They offered encouragement and sound advice during one long hot summer. I thank Tom Evans for his editorial help and typing. And I am grateful to Vivienne George and to the librarians of California State University, Chico, for their tireless assistance. Finally, I thank all those who have aided and cheered me along the way.

CHERI DAVIS

University of Leicester
Leicester, England

Acknowledgments

For quotations from copyrighted material I have been granted permission by the following: Mary Slowik and the Graduate College of the University of Iowa for Mary Slowik's "The Loss That Has Not Left This Place: The Problem of Form in the Poetry of W. S. Merwin"; The Macmillan Company for W. B. Yeats's "A Coat"; and Atheneum Publishers for W. S. Merwin's "Choice of Prides," "Economy," and "Memory of Spring."

List of Abbreviations

The following is a legend of the abbreviations to be used in the text:

AN *Animae*. San Francisco: Kayak, 1969.

AF *Asian Figures*. New York: Atheneum, 1973.

CL *The Carrier of Ladders*. New York: Atheneum, 1970.

C *The Compass Flower*. New York: Atheneum, 1977.

F *The First Four Books*. New York: Atheneum, 1975.

H *Houses and Travellers*. New York: Atheneum, 1977.

L *The Lice*. New York: Atheneum, 1967.

MJ *A Mask for Janus*. New Haven: Yale University Press, 1952.

MP *The Miner's Pale Children*. New York: Atheneum, 1970.

MT *The Moving Target*. New York: Atheneum, 1963.

O "On Open Form." In *The New Naked Poetry*. Eds. Stephen Berg and Robert Mezey. Indianapolis: Bobbs-Merrill, 1976, pp. 276–78.

ST *Selected Translations 1948–1968*. New York: Atheneum, 1969.

W *Writings to an Unfinished Accompaniment*. New York: Atheneum, 1973.

Chronology

1927   William Stanley Merwin born in New York City, September 30, son of a Presbyterian minister. He is descended from Miles Merwin, who sailed from Milford Haven to Boston in 1630. Childhood in Union City, New Jersey, and Scranton, Pennsylvania.

1944– Attends Princeton University. College career interrupted for a
1947   year by a stint in the U.S. Navy Air Corps.

1948   Graduates from Princeton with a degree in romance languages and spends one year in the Princeton Graduate School studying modern languages and doing translations of French and Spanish literature.

1949   Tutors in France and Portugal.

1950   Tutors Robert Graves's son in Majorca.

1951– Lives in London working as a translator of French and Spanish
1954   classics for the British Broadcasting Corporation.

1952   First volume of poems, *A Mask for Janus*, published with a Foreword by W. H. Auden as ninth book in the Yale Younger Poets Series.

1954   Marries Diana Whalley. Publishes *The Dancing Bears*.

1956   A play in verse, *Darkling Child*, written with Dido Milroy, is produced at the Arts Theatre in London. Returns to America to write plays for the Poets' Theatre, Cambridge, Massachusetts. Receives a Rockefeller Playwriting Fellowship. *Green with Beasts* published.

1957   A play, *Favor Island*, produced at the Poets' Theatre. Receives a National Institute of Arts and Letters Grant and Arts Council of Great Britain Playwriting Bursary.

1958   Translates Lope Felix de Vega Carpio's *Punishment Without Vengeance*.

1959   Translates and publishes *The Poem of the Cid*.

1960   Publishes *The Drunk in the Furnace*.

1961– Poetry Editor for *The Nation*. During this period translates
1963   *The Satires of Persius* (1961), *Some Spanish Ballads* (1961), *The Life of Lazarillo de Tormes: His Fortunes and Adversities* (1962), and *The Song of Roland* (1963).

1963   *The Moving Target.* Lives with his second wife Dido Milroy
       in New York City and on their farm near Lot, France. Receives
       a Rabinowitz Foundation Grant.

1964– Associated for ten months with Roger Planchon's Théâtre de la
1965   Cîté in Lyons, France. Receives a Ford Foundation Grant and
       the 1964 Kenyon Review Fellowship in Poetry.

1966   Receives a Chapelbrook Foundation Fellowship.

1967   Wins Harriet Monroe Memorial Prize and publishes *The Lice.*

1969   Receives Rockefeller Foundation Grant. *Selected Translations
       1948–1968* wins the P.E.N. Prize for Translation. A chapbook
       Animae published by Kayak Press.

1970   *The Carrier of Ladders, The Miner's Pale Children* (short
       prose pieces), and *Signs,* illustrated by A. D. Moore, published.
       Translates Pablo Neruda's *Twenty Poems of Love and a Song
       of Despair.*

1971   Wins the Pulitzer Prize for *The Carrier of Ladders.* Divides his
       time between his farmhouse in Lot, France, and an old house
       he refurbishes in San Cristóbal de las Casas, Chiapas, Mexico.

1973   Publishes *Writings to an Unfinished Accompaniment* and
       Asian Figures (Asian translations). Awarded the Fellowship of
       the Academy of American Poets. Translates, with Clarence
       Brown, *Osip Mandelstam: Selected Poems.*

1975   *The First Four Books of Poems,* a collection of his first four
       books of poetry, published.

1977   Publishes *Sanskrit Love Poetry,* translated in collaboration with
       J. Moussaieff Masson, and *Vertical Poetry,* the translated poetry
       of Roberto Juarroz. Also publishes *The Compass Flower* and
       Houses and Travellers (prose).

1978   Translates *Euripides: Iphigeneia at Aulis* with George E.
       Dimock, Jr. Lives in Haiku, Hawaii, with Dana Naone, but fre-
       quently travels across the United States giving poetry readings.

1979   *Selected Translations 1968–1978.* Wins Yale University
       Library's Bollingen Prize in Poetry.

CHAPTER 1

Voyager in the Spaces of the Poem

Prologue

PLACING W. S. Merwin in the context of contemporary American poetry is challenging. True to the tradition of Emerson's American Scholar, he pursues his own path, the road not taken. In "Air" from *The Moving Target,* he writes:

> Naturally it is night.
> Under the overturned lute with its
> One string I am going my way
> Which has a strange sound.
>
> This way the dust, that way the dust.
> I listen to both sides
> But keep right on. . . .
>
> This must be what I wanted to be doing,
> Walking at night between the two deserts,
> Singing. (MT, 50)

This is a statement of his individualism: his poetic voice is the "overturned lute with its / One string." His way "has a strange sound," but is his own way. One of his favorite aphorisms by Antonio Porchia in the *Voices* collection he translated is: "They will say that you are on the wrong road, if it is your own."[1]

In *The Iowa Review* (1970) Ralph J. Mills, Jr., grouped Merwin among those poets who have a "kind of openness—a sensitive receptivity in which the poet, to borrow a phrase of Heidegger's about Holderlin, 'is exposed to divine lightnings.'" In an analysis still valid today of this kind of poet, Mills argues that this openness is a visionary openness:

[It] extends, in many instances beyond matters of social and political experience to naked metaphysical confrontation: with the universe, the identity of the self, the possibilities of an absent or present God, or the prospect of a vast, overwhelming nothingness. In such poets as Theodore Roethke, Kenneth Patchen, John Berryman, Robert Lowell, James Wright, Anne Sexton, James Dickey, W. S. Merwin, and the late Sylvia Plath, for example, with all difference aside, the pursuit of personal vision often leads toward a precipitous, dizzying boundary where the self stands alone, unaided but for its own resources, before the seemingly tangible earth at hand with its bewildering multiplicity of life, the remoteness of space, the endless rhythms of nature, the turns of night and day, and within, the elusive images of memory and dream, the irrationality and uncertainty of human behavior, the griefs and ecstasies that living accumulates.[2]

As a result of its "naked metaphysical confrontation" with the earth and its creatures, the Promethean self crafts a world out of its own personal vision. The boundaries between self and the non-self sometimes fall away ("Which I is *I*?"), and the soul—as Theodore Roethke puts it—is set "free in the tearing wind."[3] In the short poem "Laughter," Merwin writes: "The great gods are blind or pretend to be / finding that I am among men I open my eyes / and they shake" (CL, 68).

Another way of placing Merwin might be to say that he follows the literary tradition of Romanticism. Speaking of Merwin's poem "Whenever I Go There," Robert Pinsky writes:

Dream, art, or meditation, the process he uses to get "there" must be described as Romantic: it involves silence, and taking on (or in) that aspect of unreflecting animals, and it is named by reference not to thought, or even to action, but to the natural—and unreflecting—act of eating ["I go my way eating the silence of animals / Offering snow to the darkness. . . ."] This is Keats' "already with thee": the unconsidering mind in the unconsidering landscape.

So, in a sense, this poem embodies an extreme Romanticism: a pursuit of darkness, of silence, of the soul moving in ways so unlike abstract thought that it burrows into or "eats" its immobile paradise.[4]

Merwin pursues the darker vein of the Romantic tradition, the vein represented by Keats's "Ode to a Nightingale" and Wordsworth's Lucy poems. Unquestioning acceptance of perception, a receptivity to the Other, joy in the pursuit of what approaches a religious experience of consummation, and selflessness in the face of the majesty of nature all characterize this vein of Romanticism.

To the extent that Merwin's work has affinities with those poets we identify with specific schools of contemporary American poetry, he comes closest to Robert Bly, James Wright, Galway Kinnell, and the Deep Imagists,[5] in his creation of a series of complex poetic images emanating from the depths of the psyche, often never emerging into consciousness in the poems. Merwin's unquestioning acceptance of perception serves paradoxically to call into question the very structure of perception as it is traditionally understood. In this he is like the poets named above. In his work the images often remain deeply submerged, awaiting the reader's intuitive, if not intellectual resolution. The reader climbs around amid the words, pauses, and images as one climbs rocks underwater; one is never certain where the next step will carry him. But Merwin is more spiritual and less down-to-earth than the Deep Imagists.

Today it is a commonplace to point out that most poets who began their careers in the late 1940s and early to mid-1950s started out writing technically controlled, formalist poetry rhetorically imitative of the poetry of Ezra Pound's *Des Imagistes* period, or the early T. S. Eliot. Robert Lowell's *Lord Weary's Castle,* awarded the Pulitzer Prize in 1946, and *The Mills of the Kavanaughs* (1951) were models for this generation; it then experienced a revolution in sensibility in the 1960s. The generation started experimenting in open forms. Tightly controlled rhyme schemes, meters, and forms disappeared. In their wake came a diversification in forms and poetic voices, more personal revelation, more particularizing of events, dates, place, persons, a sharpening of the focus, a movement inward. Lowell's "Skunk Hour" displays the kind of daring—psychic and poetic—and the kind of personal revelation that characterizes the generation's new expansiveness and courageous candor. But while other poets of his generation may add an obscure reference or a bit of color merely to contribute a hint of the bizarre to the poem, Merwin is more apt to achieve a shocking effect by leading the reader to contemplate the horror of the void at the very center of his own placid, conventional ideas about life and experience. He admits the reader into the poem, then disappears, leaving one looking into a mirror which reflects back one's self-deceptions. His brief poem "Economy" goes: "No need to break the mirror. / Here is the face shattered, / Good for seven years of sorrow" (MT, 13).

Silence and an awareness of the mystery or silence of life are major themes in Merwin's poetry and prose. At the end of *The Moving Target*, he writes: "The future woke me with its silence / I join the proces-

sion" (97). Silence is what is being masked in *A Mask for Janus:* it is
the underside of the elaborate edifice of language he builds in the first
two books. In 1958, in the poem "The Drunk in the Furnace," later
published in the book by that name, Merwin began to explore the
depths of that silence by venturing to admit its existence. The dead
furnace which experiences a "Resurrection" in the poem is the depth
of his own poetic individuality beginning to be tapped. The unlit furnace is "the tar-paper church" which will be the center of his spiritual
investigations: "Where he gets his spirits / It's a mystery" (F, 261).
Going deeper into the dark void of the furnace of silence is proceeding
deeper into the raw material of the psyche, the terrible realm of chaos.
In attempting to deal directly with the raw stuff of the imagination,
working at the place before "the names of things existed," Merwin
moves "in a resolutely elliptical way from image to atomistic
image. . . . Perception is more to be trusted than reflection, former
ideas are obstacles, and the large, blank, irreducible phenomena are
the truest incarnations of reality."[6] The "large, blank, irreducible phenomena" might be analogized to the sides of the inner furnace of his
real poetic voice. The voice had been effaced in his earlier attempts to
conform to the prevailing poetic style.[7]

Robert Pinsky sees Merwin's major impact on contemporary writing
today in the areas of diction, manner, and style. Speaking of Merwin's
inclination to create "a generic experience" through the use of a
generic diction, Pinsky says, "because the style is so distinctly identi-
fiable, it is liable to be taken . . . as a kind of *lingua franca,* divorced
from the philosophical inclinations which give the style its coherence
and integrity."[8] He is concerned that a third-rate imitation of the style
may become the new exemplar for beginning poets. But Pinsky over-
looks the function of silence as a communicator of meaning in Merwin's poetry. After all, poetry inheres as much in the silences, the profound interstices between lines as it does in the words themselves.
Though a young poet might succeed in imitating Merwin's diction, he
could never imitate his silences. Merwin has called silence "our first
language." And of the lack of specificity even in particular names, he
writes, "how many things come to one name / hoping to be fed (CL,
131)."

The absolute toward which Merwin's poetry moves as it progresses
through the 1960s and into the 1970s is not merely negation, though
it includes negation, the obliteration of all value and even of personal
identity. Paradoxically, the absolute can only be approached and stated

by virtue of negation. Loss of the individual self's ego furnishings is the risk one must take, the loss one must accept as poet today. One moves into the realm of Keats's negative capability, seeking to describe things in terms of what they are *not:* "my love outlined in knives." It is a negative aesthetic Merwin formulates. As Sandra McPherson expressed it in 1973, "There is an art to writing in the negative just as writing affirmatively is an art. Once in a while a poet builds his style on his use of denials. W. S. Merwin is one of these poets. 'The Owl' is about '*You who are* never there.'" Each negative image is an approach to the void, an attempt at approximating it in language.

If this void is frightening and if death, the ultimate, is the great American obscenity, it is natural that American critics would be repulsed by Merwin's lack of self-consciousness, of hardy ego-defensiveness in confrontation with death and with other voids that are more spiritual. Nor is it surprising that McPherson criticizes the language of these images as vague: "He is researching the erasures of the universe . . . I felt he chose vague words to describe the vague, mysterious phrases to evoke the mysterious."[9] How could one speak of the unknown specifically? In Merwin's work things come to "Appear / not as they are / but as what prevents them?" (CL, 118)

In summary, Merwin is a visionary poet whose work reflects an engagement in the silence of the self, a receptivity to supranatural experiences, and, in the later work, an openness to participation in the lives of other creatures, and a questioning of the basic structures of perception. In pursuing the negative aesthetic, he opens the way for a poetry that is mystical without being effusive, intimate without being personal, formal without taking itself (or anything or anyone else) too seriously, a poetry that is inspired yet controlled in that it follows a regular, if elliptical, pattern of thought.

II *Personal and Poetic Origins*

> And the end of all our exploring
> Will be to arrive where we started
> And know the place for the first time.
>   T. S. Eliot, "Little Gidding"

Beginning as a scholar of romance languages and of the literature of the Middle Ages while an undergraduate at Princeton, this Presbyterian minister's son soon dedicated himself to the craft of verse and

engaged in writing dark pagan accounts of fateful sea voyages and
anabases. At the outset, W. S. Merwin establishes himself as one of the
best poetic craftsmen alive; he is intelligent, facile, and capable of con-
siderable feats with traditional rhymes and verse forms. His early work
produces the impression that one is reading a poet of advanced years
at the peak of his poetic capability. Its tone is dry, satiric, sophisticated.
Sestinas, villanelles, roundels, songs, carols, masques, even mad songs
in the manner of W. B. Yeats's Crazy Jane attract the young Merwin's
attention and prowess. He masters each successive taxing form easily
and moves on to try his skill with the next. As the stiff elaboration of
the verses increases, so does the remoteness from life, from the natural
and human spheres.

In the course of his thirty-year career, Merwin has displayed a thor-
oughly professional mastery of poetic form and diction as well as a
dexterity at assuming one poetic style after another, as Yeats did.
Movement forward into new adventures and new challenges is one
constant of his career. Another constant is his preoccupation with
myth. He sees myth as a cultural repository for spiritual and philosophical information about human beings and the human character.
The constellation of myths implies a structure, in essence, even a creed
of law for living. He uses the mythological heritage as given laws of
life. The traditional order of myth presented a ready-made order to
the young, educated poet who wanted to connect himself and his work
with "the best which has been known and thought in the world." By
writing new versions of the Greek and Biblical myths Merwin reinter-
prets the old tales for our time and makes compelling, if veiled, statements about his own culture. Thus, at the onset, W. S. Merwin is a poet
who is vividly aware of the inherited corpus of the literature of belief
and who himself seeks to write a literature of belief.

Having mastered the panoply of medieval verse forms, by 1956
Merwin was a practicing playwright and holder of a Rockefeller Playwriting Fellowship. In his only published play, *Favor Island*, the narrator voices this assessment of man:

> Part beast, part shadow, tracks and flees
> Beasts and shadows round their valleys
> Outdoing both their cruelties
> Comes to much harm, some rightly his,
> And yet endures, and on the darkness
> Still sires his changeless miseries,
> His singular and painful glories.[10]

This wry, mystical view of the human being as part beast and part shadow or spirit undergirds the poetry of *A Mask for Janus* (1952) and *The Dancing Bears* (1954). His view of the human character is all the more interesting when one takes into account the fact that Merwin and his forebear Ralph Waldo Emerson see dreams and beasts as the keys to the kingdom of the imagination and to the "underworld." They impart information about the origins of mankind—its collective psyche and collective unconsciousness. He believes that to a large extent "We are such stuff as dreams are made on." This belief marks both the limitations and the strengths of the man and the poet. Accomplished as spinner of imaginative constructs, he has, unlike Shakespeare, no gift for delineating character traits or unique personalities. Instead, he is an acidic observer of society's ills and human folly, the ideal translator of *The Satires of Persius*.

The setting of his first two volumes of poetry is inconceivably far from the squalid community of Merwin's origin, Union City, New Jersey. He was born in New York City on September 30, 1927; but he grew up in Union City (the subject of many of the initial poems in *The Moving Target*) and in Scranton, Pennsylvania. In 1947, he was graduated from Princeton University; his university career had been interrupted by a period of service in the U.S. Navy Air Corps.

Perhaps because he was living through times of great international upheaval, he was drawn to the stability and certainty of the medieval epics, which he subsequently translated and to which he alludes in the poem "Teachers" as "sure tellings that do not start by justifying." The bravery, honor, and high style of the literature of the Middle Ages deeply appealed to Merwin.

After graduation from Princeton, Merwin travelled to Europe where from 1949 to 1951 he worked as a tutor in France, Portugal, and Majorca. When he published his first volume of poetry, *A Mask for Janus* (1952), he had served for a year as tutor to Robert Graves's son and had assimilated and made his own Graves's passion for mythology and ancient history.[11] Evidences of this passion are everywhere in the poetry: "Suspicor Speculum"—"I shall raise the stone"—is dedicated, for example, to Sysyphus, and he writes two anabases, echoing Xenophon, and "Ode: The Medusa Face."

Because of its world-weary mood, Merwin's poetry of this period sounds like the poetry of an old man. The poet's own evaluation of his early books is that they reveal "influence, through Pound, of the Middle Ages. I was laboring under some notion of poetry, based as much as anything on notions in Pound's Mauberley, and Yeats. Romanticism of a kind, clearly, though I thought of myself as very unromantic, and in a way, was."[12] Certainly this choice of models would account for the strict formalism of *A Mask for Janus* and *The Dancing Bears*.

It is probably correct to assume that Merwin found a grace and elegance in the Middle Ages that was lacking in contemporary America of the post-war years. In transposing himself into the Middle Ages in his poetry, he was rejecting, as Eliot and Pound did, the gracelessness of the current age. A yearning for a past age of purity and courage is one method of escaping—and passing negative judgment on—the present.

After *A Mask for Janus*, two more books of poetry followed at two-year intervals, They were *The Dancing Bears* (1954), whose title is taken from a statement in Flaubert's *Madame Bovary*, "human language is like a cracked cauldron whereon we beat out melodies to make bears dance, when we wish to have compassion of the stars," and *Green with Beasts* (1956), whose title is taken from his own poem "Two Horses": "But in the night green with beasts as April with grass / Orion would hunt high from southward, . . ." (F, 131). The poet's urge to reach for stars underlies each title.

Four years later Merwin published *The Drunk in the Furnace* (1960) which, like *Green with Beasts*, is a compilation of long, conversational poems. But the poetry of *The Drunk in the Furnace* is more objective and realistic than any of his previous work. With its preoccupation with the sea, interminable voyages, and Odyssean journey, it has a darker, more futile vision than *Green with Beasts*.

To those accustomed to the regular poetic rectangles and neatly aligned stanzas of his two former volumes, Merwin's *The Moving Target* (1963) came as a surprise. Its form is jagged, bare, slashed open form. Gone is Merwin's early semblance of objectivity. This volume and his four subsequent volumes of poetry, *The Lice* (1967), *The Carrier of Ladders* (1970), *Writings to an Unfinished Accompaniment* (1973), and *The Compass Flower* (1977), are in his new style: they display a characteristic blunt verbal economy and a matte poetic surface. In 1971, Merwin won the Pulitzer Prize for *The Carrier of Ladders*.

By avocation Merwin is a translator of poetry: for over thirty years he has been reading and translating French and Spanish poetry, not as his main life's work, but as a diversion from his own poetry. Merwin writes in his Foreword to *Selected Translations 1948–1968:* "The great exemplar, of course, was Pound. The neo-Flaubertian image of poetry as a craft was in all the ikons I could see."[13] Following Pound's advice and example, then, he proceeded to embody the spirit of the Middle Ages in his earliest poems, much as Pound had in *Personae* and *A Lume Spento*, and as James Joyce had in *Pomes Pennyeach*. But even more rigorously than Pound or Joyce, Merwin practiced the old verse forms until he achieved consummate mastery of them. He became a collector of archaisms: words like "perduring," "bourn," "euphory," and "darkling" figure in his poetry (as they do in Robert Lowell's poetry of the 1940s and 1950s). An archaic abstraction will occasionally be linked with a familiar word, as in the phrase "euphory and afternoon." This seeking a shocking effect through juxtaposition of the recondite with the contemporary is further evidence of Pound's influence. Indeed, Richard Howard has commented that "the pair of poems called *Anabases* in their slant rhymes and many slack endings, their deceptively neat-looking quatrains and languid rhythms, suggest a St.-John Perse rewritten by Hugh Selwyn Mauberley."[14] Certainly Mauberley was nothing if not a disciple of Flaubert, emphasizing as he did the capacity of style to sustain a work of art.

Correspondingly, style takes precedence over meaning in "Anabasis" I and II. These poems may defy all but the most astute readers, yet the sway and current of their style, the delight in Merwin's apt and artful diction afford a lush pleasure. The final quatrain of "Anabasis II" rings of Pound's "Hugh Selwyn Mauberley," though it lacks Pound's chiseled clarity: "Still we are strange to orisons and knees. / Fixed to bone only, foreign as we came, / We float leeward till mind and body lose / The uncertain continent of a name" (F, 9). Just as "Hugh Selwyn Mauberley" is a repudiation of the crass, hyperactive modern age, Merwin's "Anabasis II" is a denial of the American character. Its narrator renounces even the traditional consolations of home, family, and religion: "we are strange to orisons and knees." With pagan endurance and stoicism, he faces certain death at sea and its consequent oblivion.

III   *Myth in the Early Poetry*

Any serious student of *A Mask for Janus* will do well to read W. H. Auden's Foreword to it first. Regrettably, this Foreword is not reproduced in Atheneum's edition of the *The First Four Books*. It appears only in the Yale University Press 1952 edition of the book. In the

Foreword, a short laudatory piece introducing Merwin to the poetry-reading public, Auden establishes the young Merwin's reputation as a superior craftsman and intrepreter of myth: "With his concern for the traditional conceptions of Western culture as expressed in its myths, Mr. Merwin combines an admirable respect for its traditions of poetic craftsmanship."[15]

Auden distinguishes between two kinds of poetry being written. The first kind, the kind we might today characterize as confessional or occasional poetry, Auden describes thus: "The overt subject of the poem is a specific experience undergone by the 'I' of the poem at a specific time and place." Conversely, "in the second kind, the overt subject is universal and impersonal, frequently a myth, and it is the personal experience of the poet which is implied" (p. vii). Auden continues his analysis of the modern scene, emphasizing that the second kind of poetry is probably preferable to the first. By way of justification he states: "the profundity and eternal relevance to the human condition of the great myths cannot fail to instill the most immature writer who reflects upon them with that reverence and wonder without which no man can become wise" (p. viii). By implication Auden asserts that Merwin possesses this "reverence and wonder," that he is indeed wise. Heady praise for a poet barely twenty-five years old! Auden then proceeds to discuss "Dictum: For a Masque of Deluge," a poem based on the myth of the Flood, illustrating the excellence of the work.

Alice Benston has argued that Merwin insists "on myth-making as a creative process by which existence is reduced from chaos to order through the ordering principle of language itself."[16] Both myth and language structure reality, dispelling the chaos of unexamined experience. Myth derives its authority both from tradition and from the fact that it is a ritual enactment of man's experience on this earth. As such, it provides a way of understanding the diversity and range of human experience.

Both myth and language have taproots in the living cultural heritage. Myth is a timeless record of man's most private observations about himself and his own nature: it participates in the collective psyche of mankind and in the collective unconscious. Myth presents the modern writer with a monolithic, traditional order, readily accessible to the poet who is attracted to embodying some of the world's profoundest assessments of human nature in his art. As Auden stressed, the poet working with myth—biblical and otherwise—avoids getting caught in the pitfall of attributing undue significance to seemingly major current events. Absorption in myth turns the poet's focus inward and makes it universal.

Cast in ritual order in language, myth is the last surviving remnant of Graeco-Roman religion. Containing fragments of beliefs, it carries with it some of the conviction of religion without carrying the attendant necessity for belief. Its mode of existence as part fiction, part sacrament, intrigues Merwin. Benston defines mythic reality as it manifests itself in his early poetry thus: "Fundamentally, Merwin views reality as an inchoate mass of possibilities, of a chaos fraught with alternatives and populated by shadows that have substance—a reality which is grasped through belief and through the pronouncement of that belief. An unstated first line that the reader comes to hear behind the poems is the New Testament's 'In the beginning was the word.' This emphasis on the word, on the necessity as well as the creative power of language, is constantly stressed in Merwin's first two volumes, *A Mask for Janus,* and *The Dancing Bears,* where metaphors based on language are pervasive."[17] The creative force of the word holds down the inchoate flux of reality and itself constructs reality. The creative force of the word is highly intriguing to this young poet immersed in the Blackmur school of New Criticism.

Moreover, Merwin does not merely write new versions of the extant myths: he turns myths in upon themselves, making them self-reflexive. As Benston puts it:

> What is fascinating about Merwin's use of myth is that he goes well beyond the retelling of old fables (old wine in new bottles) and, as an artist, seems to take myth as a creed. Thus the element of Romantic self-consciousness is part of his poetry. For when the subject is the myth itself, we are at the beginnings, at creation. And when we are dealing with a creation which is continuous, that is, when the nature of the act is stressed rather than the specific accomplishment, we are concerned with the creator, who must either be God or the artist. Merwin's emphasis on this aspect of modern myth-making is certainly in the tradition established by the Romantics.[18]

The poet thus conceives of himself as having Promethean powers. Perpetually creative on a scale approaching that of divine creativity, he is also perpetually self-conscious, and this self-consciousness is traceable in his art. In "East of the Sun, West of the Moon," Merwin's Cupid and Psyche myth, Psyche asks of herself: "And what am I if the story be not real?" (F, 89) With her query the poem becomes self-reflective for the first time, self-aware of its own predetermined fictive existence.

Likewise in Merwin's embodiment of a myth "Proteus," the narrator/protagonist wrestles Proteus to the ground, subduing him after an heroic struggle, only to find that "The head he turned toward me wore a face of mine" (F, 102). It is impossible for the creator imaging himself in his poetry to get away from himself. Solipsism is the trap of the self-reflective work of art. Perhaps this is the reason that the myths Merwin chooses to embody are models of human fallibility: he recreates myths of disaster—Paris's judgment of the three goddesses who brought on the Trojan War, the myth of the Flood, the stories of Medusa, and Sisyphus. All his mythic heroes prove to be less than heroic. His recreations have, then, a subtle didactic basis in that they are warnings: they show us the smug preconceptions we are to avoid. Indeed, he indicates that we are *not* "assured of certain certainties," but that life must be created and understood afresh each day.

Merwin's "earliest and most constant insight" is one he shares with Joyce and Jung: it is that "people live in stories that structure their worlds" and that all stories are but "the one story rotated."[19] One cannot step outside the glass shell of one's own believing; one cannot move out of his preconceptions, which structure reality so that it fits the pattern of his story; therefore, the poet sees his "characters" as determined, almost condemned, to live out the "stories"—stories they perceive as real. At any point there is of course the possibility that the character will achieve a new level of self-consciousness and will alter the fated events so that the outcome may finally be victorious rather than disastrous. Therein lies the suspense in Merwin's early narratives.

IV   Form: Chaos vs. Order

In a Princeton undergraduate essay on classical French drama, Merwin explored aesthetic contrasts between Racine and Corneille, noting especially their differing manners of coming to grips with the potential chaos which underlies rational human conduct. Working from T. E. Hulme's premise that "man is the chaos highly organized but liable to revert to chaos, at any moment," Merwin understands Corneille "as concerning himself principally with the means and possibilties of organization and Racine with the inevitability and suddenness of reversion." Richard Howard deduces from this that we "might properly call Merwin's early work Corneillean, and the later books Racinian."[20]

My focus in this section will be specifically on the Corneillean aspects of Merwin's early books, A *Mask for Janus* and *The Dancing*

Bears. The dialectic confrontation between chaos and control engages Merwin here; he sees form as an indispensable ordering principle of poetry, in fact as the salvation of poetry. In the years at Princeton and the anti-intellectual early fifties of his first publications, poetic form became for the young Merwin a means of firmly and irreversibly ordering the external and internal worlds, welding them together, for a moment at least, in perfect harmony.

In a passage significant for his own work, Merwin discusses the dynamics of chaos and control in an early essay on classical French drama: "The necessity, the provocations, the concerns of disintegration are seen most clearly where the original order was most nearly complete. We cannot proceed simply to consider the organization as specious. A false order would not contain but be its own process of reversion. A judgment of any order will involve considerations of how much is contained in balance, of how strong the form can remain, while allowing all possible variations."[21] His interest here is in the *nearly* completed form in which the void is about to wake and expand, possibly encompassing the whole. He perceives that where the formal order is most stringently controlled and fixed, there is the greatest temptation to break the discipline of that order.

Something in the language of Merwin's expression of this idea recalls the literature of the Christian mystics, men and women who were equally drawn to and repulsed by thoughts of sin. And it is in the Christian tradition that Merwin is writing, though God and dogma have departed from his theological sphere. Christian myth and the Christian fellowship between man and nature remain. Several poems from each of his published books are reweavings of Biblical myths. His poems place man at the center of creation. In Merwin's work man is indeed master of all things, yet this position of mastery devolves in the later books into a hollow, lonely dominance. At times man imagines himself "cold as the thoughts of birds," stuck up on a naked promontory like a totem animal, delivering prophecies which none can fathom, trying to help but failing.

Merwin struggles with the problem of how best to use his poetic gift. He always conceived of the poet's mission as carrying with it heavy responsibilities, responsibilities like Noah's or Prometheus' for the welfare of the animals and mankind: "It is possible for a poet to assume his gift of articulation as a responsibility not only to the fates but to his neighbors, and to feel himself obliged to try to speak for those who are in circumstances resembling his own. . . ."[22] Such a poet is, of course, a human being endowed with conscience, a human being of integrity. Hence the necessity for the stringent formal discipline and controlled articulation of the Provençal verse forms of the early books: if the poet is to speak for his race, Merwin assumes he must speak in an exemplary, traditional manner. Still, one senses that Merwin is, along with Racine, a connoisseur of chaos. He perceives the logic of Wallace Stevens's statements in "Connoisseur of Chaos": "A violent order is disorder; and / A great disorder is an order." Merwin knows that the challenges he faces are all within, in the immense silence of the self.

Could it be that beneath the rigid formal order of his poetry lurks a violent disorder? It is possible that without the elaborate verse forms, there could be no poetry, for the chaos of which he speaks in his essay would engulf and obliterate the rational human order. All the same, in adopting this high formal style he is behaving as befits a young craftsman learning to exercise his craft.

The concept of poetic form is closely linked with hearing in Merwin's thought. In his only published notes on form he gives the following definition of form: "A poetic form: the setting down of a way of hearing how poetry happens in words. The words themselves do not make it. At the same time it is testimony of a way of hearing how life happens in time. But time does not make it." He goes on to say: "At the same time I realize that I am a formalist, in the most strict and orthodox sense. For years I have had a recurring dream of finding, as it were in an attic, poems of my own that were as lyrically formal, but as limpid and essentially unliterary as those of Villon." This articulates his "composer's" view of form: it should be "lyrically formal," classical in the manner of the medieval French poet Villon, yet "limpid and essentially unliterary." His notion is of an unpretentious, clear, lyrical elegance. In all his writing Merwin seeks a musical clarity, a "resonance, something that is repeating no sound." (O, 278)

In the poems of W. S. Merwin, Wallace Stevens, and W. B. Yeats, the word for poetry is always "song." In A Mask for Janus, no fewer than nine poems have "carol," "song," or "cancion" in their titles, while in The Dancing Bears there are eight poems so titled, three of which are simply "Canso." Discussing his apprenticeship at the harmonium of language in a poem dedicated to Robert Graves, Merwin assesses his youth thus: "I woke with new words, and in every place, / Under different lights, evening and morning, / Under many masters studied one song" (F, 43).

V   *The Relationship between Love and Belief*
in the Early Poetry

Both love and the poem are believed into existence in Merwin's early
work. He treats the nature of poetic belief in this stanza from "Canso":

> Say it is the idea of a place
> That has no imagination of its own;
> Yet in these nothing-fertile notions of
> Valleys, . . .
> And the actual lake moving its metaphor
> Under real birds conceived, although conceived
> Only for uses elsewhere. It is between
> These twin antinomies that I must walk
> Casting, it seems, no image; between these poles
> Of vanity I must make you real. (F, 115)

The passage has the typical conversational beginning Stevens often
employed, and Merwin's depiction of "a place / That has no imagination of its own" invokes the Tennessee dominated by the jar in Wallace Stevens's "Anecdote of a Jar." The imagination crafts and forms
nature, infusing it with meaning. In Merwin's "Canso" nature is sometimes passive: "these nothing-fertile notions of / Valleys, this static
nature." But nature also has motion and dynamic activity—"the actual
lake moving." It is between these "antinomies" that the poet walks, an
alien, "Casting, it seems, no image; between these poles / Of vanity
that I must make you real." Both the static and dynamic aspects of
nature are conceived as opposing vanities. As in Keats's "Ode to a
Nightingale," only the song, the resonance of the imagination, is real.

In "Canso," when his lady asks the source of the poet's impulse to
create, the poet responds: "Lady, you know. Creation waits upon / The
word; but you in silence are the conception / And the consent of
speech, the metaphor / In the midst of chaos, whose word is love" (F,
117). Love is here imagined as a kind of divine fiat which impels creation. In its realm of belief all that it establishes is true in perpetuity;
in this realm her word, the single correct word, unlocks the doors of
perception. Love, like art, dispels chaos and orders the raw materials
nature provides.

The poet/lover proceeds, echoing St. Paul: "though I had / Imagi-
nations to remove mountains / Out of their shadows, and did not have

this love, / I were a vain instrument: I were nothing" (F, 117–18). There is no disputing the sovereignty of this *Logos*-like love. Without it the creator could not infuse his poems with spirit substance and being, though he had the proverbial faith that moves mountains. This love, this word, then, holds the imperatives for all formal order, restraint, decorum, and true understanding. Without love he would be "a vain instrument" like the sounding gong or clanging cymbal, his words lacking conviction or intelligible meaning, the poems lacking formal completeness or coherence.

Excitement over the clarifying, creative power of the word animates Merwin's early work. The Gnostic conception that the creator's talent or inventiveness acquires a magical dimension, that there is a single secret to the universe, and that the poet, like Einstein solving the riddles of relativity, can and will find this secret by means of the perfect word—all these ideas are implicit in the poem "Canso" and other early poems. In his discussion of the myth of Einstein, Roland Barthes gives the following analysis of the Gnostic system of belief: "In it we find all the Gnostic themes: the unity of nature, the ideal possibility of a fundamental reduction of the world, the unfastening power of the word, the age-old struggle between a secret and an utterance, the idea that total knowledge can only be discovered all at once."[23]

Just as the popular mind conceived Albert Einstein as a genius about to write what Barthes calls "the magic formula of the world," so Merwin envisions the ideal poet as one who penetrates, in Promethean fashion, to the source of truth and apprehends all knowledge by virtue of his love, which is, like the philosophers' stone, a vehicle of transformation and metamorphosis. Constant search and research for the word, which is love, thus engages him. Each new love, "believing, names a new paradigm"—a new paradise. Each is a new *logos,* echoing *his* story, "In the beginning was the word." With its coming into being the world begins anew: "And your believing spins continually / Its own newness: . . . // It is by your faith that I believe, I am" (F, 110). I believe, therefore I am. What better rephrasing of Descartes to express the essence of the Christian message? Given the firm Biblical grounding of Merwin's poetry, the highly original reworking of traditional Christian themes, and his precocious technical achievement, it is not surprising that W. H. Auden concluded that *A Mask for Janus* had "an assumed authority." The preserve of *A Mask for Janus* is an Eden of elegance and eloquence, an ornate fortress standing fast against the potential onslaughts of the "process of reversion," a place containing the Tree of Life as well as the Tree of Knowledge, the snake as well as the apple. Merwin's hallmark is control; his control over language, meter, rhyme, and form is at once the mask and the triumph of his poetry. In "East of the Sun, West of the Moon": "I walk multifarious among / My baubles and horses; unless I go in a mask / How shall I know myself among my faces?" (F, 99) The impersonal mask of the high formal style is necessary to cover the protean changes in the young poet's psyche, which varies like the metaphors he creates.

VI *Wallace Stevens, W. S. Merwin and the Poetry of Belief*

Like Robert Frost, who sees each poem as "a momentary stay against confusion," Wallace Stevens views writing poetry as an entrance into the unfamiliar, inchoate realm where thought, emotion, and sensation combine in a welter that is the raw substance of the poem. Stevens asserts that writing poetry is "the act of becoming engaged with something unreal."[24] Merwin also views the act of writing a poem as an entrance into a psychic state where all is incipient, unformed, and unknown. His art is founded on the premise that the self is knowable chiefly through the exercise of the imagination. In image-making the poet experiences his fullest life. The exercise of his rational faculties is of lesser importance to him than this creative work. Thought, emotion, the senses all nourish the poem and the self, they are vital to sustain the poet as a whole human being. In his creative labor he feels he is godlike, bringing new realities into existence where nothing existed before. Without the life of the imagination the poet could not *live*.

To satisfy and fulfill him, Merwin's imaginative mind must be constantly engaged. It must be venturing into and grappling with the unformed and unknown. On entering a higher order of reality and experiencing a heightened sense of awareness and vitality, the poet forges a poem out of the living material of consciousness. Merwin translates an aphorism by Antonio Porchia: "We tear life out of life to use it for looking at itself."[25] The poet sees into the life at the recesses of consciousness and "tears" that life out in order to see all of reality more clearly and vividly. All Merwin's poems are born of this creative impulse to fathom the unknown.

For Merwin and Stevens, as for Mallarmé and Rimbaud, reality without the vivid poetic gloss the poet writes on it is insufficient. Poetry

fulfills a religious need in these poets: poems are their spiritual expli-
cations of reality to themselves. In imagination's sight they "see the
earth again," renewed, refreshed. In *The Necessary Angel*, Stevens
says of the imagination, "We have it because we do not have enough
without it."[26] And in "Angel Surrounded by Paysans," imagination
speaks directly to the reader:

> I am the angel of reality,
> Seen for a moment standing in the door, . . .
>
> . . . I am the necessary angel of earth,
> Since, in my sight, you see the earth again,
> Cleared of its stiff and stubborn man-locked set.[27]

Imagination for Merwin, as for Stevens, is the angel necessary to
make us open our eyes and truly *see* the earth "cleared of its stiff and
stubborn man-locked set." The angel's brief visitations save us from
pedestrian literalmindedness. Still, as Stevens says in "An Ordinary
Evening in New Haven," "The poem is . . . Part of the *res* itself and
not about it." What the poet's imagination offers is his own abstraction
of the real.

Stevens considers reality and imagination to be "equal and inseparable" for the poet since in the poem and even in life they come to
resemble one another: each balances the other, each interpenetrates the
other. In the same way in "As You Leave The Room," the real and the
unreal, life and art, fact and poem come to be indentified in the mind
and in poetry—either and both are real:

> Now, here, the snow I had forgotten becomes
> Part of a major reality, part of
> An appreciation of a reality
> And thus an elevation, as if I left
> With something I could touch, touch every way
> And yet nothing has been changed except what is
> Unreal, as if nothing had been changed at all.[28]

The poet changes only what is unreal; he clears the "stiff and stubborn
man-locked set," freeing him to savor a broader perspective. As Stevens
says in "Notes Toward a Supreme Fiction,"

> The poem refreshes life so that we share,
> For a moment, the first idea . . . It satisfies

Belief in an immaculate beginning.
And sends us, winged by an unconscious will,
To an immaculate end.[29]

By refreshing life in us "so that we share . . . the first idea," the poet
feeds the human hunger for meaning. Both poets acknowledge that
institutionalized religion fails to fill their spiritual needs. Merwin
writes, "You grieve / Not that heaven does not exist but / That it exists
without us" (F, 34). Stevens believes that "Poetry / Exceeding music
must take the place, / Of empty heaven and its hymns, / Ourselves in
poetry must take their place."[30] Here in "The Man with the Blue Gui-
tar," Stevens's major poetic statement of belief, he maintains that the
poem, "a supreme fiction," can be "A substitute for all the gods . . . A
poem like a missal found / In the mud . . . / The very book, or, less,
a page."[31] These lines recall Frost's statement on the bond between
belief and poetry: "The person who gets close enough to poetry . . . is
going to know more about the word *belief* than anybody else knows,
even in religion nowadays."[32] Merwin would endorse this wholeheart-
edly. One might say that he holds this conviction so strongly and pro-
foundly that he hasn't seen the need to write about it. But that would
not be entirely true. In fact, he seldom writes criticism. However, these
stanzas from "Canso" in *The Dancing Bears* provide ample evidence
of his conviction:

But you, believing, name a new paradigm
That existed, nonetheless, before
The hour of your believing: for the order
Is, although the place where it exist
Be nowhere but a possibility; . . .

It is by your faith that I believe, I am.
Therein is genesis, as though a man,
In love with existence, should bring to belief
A divinity, an imagination
That might move upon the idea of nothing
And image a man; as though a man could make
A mirror out of his own divinity,
Wherein he might believe himself, and be. (F, 110)

He is a poet who not only finds the highest life in the life of the imagination, but who also makes "body and season from a song" (F, 43).
    In his early poetry, Merwin emphasized the imagination's ability to

soar over the mutability of earthly existence. He is aware that imagination distills and clears reality, that it is "necessary" because we cannot truly see the earth and live here appreciatively without it. He is even more strongly aware that imaginative works outlast all other products of human industry. He values them for their relative immutability. In a subsequent "Canso" he addresses the poem itself, saying that "There must be found . . . / That ceremony whereby you may be named / Perpetual out of the anonymity / Of death" (114). These final lines, their meaning reinforced by enjambment, express a major theme of the early books, immortality in art.

Although a casual reader of the first two books might conclude that one of Merwin's chief ambitions is to attain immortality in art, such a conclusion would not be wholly justified. He is more attracted to the capacity of art to immortalize the imaginative vision than in personal glory. He delights in art's escaping death: death for Stevens "is the mother of beauty," but for Merwin it is the source of all pain, the enemy of all his endeavors, craft, and skill. Still, he is too much of a cavalier to take any ambition too seriously.

To one so new to the larger sphere of national recognition, it was naturally attractive to believe fiercely in the power of one's imagination and love to defy time's encroachments, to have faith that "I, perfected in your love, may be / Against all dissolution sovereign, / Endlessly your litany and mirror" (111). Although it could not ensure sovereignty "Against all dissolution," Auden's Foreword did much to launch Merwin on the road to immortality. Certainly it set the high tone and style of Merwin criticism to follow. It established his reputation as a precocious boy wonder applauded by the most respected critic of the day.

VII   The Man Behind the Mask for Janus

W. S. Merwin comes from a family of "footloose Latin teachers," river pilots, and sailors—hardly a timid or sheltered group. Upon being awarded the Pulitzer Prize in 1971, Merwin refused to accept the prize money himself but gave it to a painter who had been blinded by police fire and to the Draft Resistance. He has made a moral commitment to abide by the dictates of his own conscience.

Following Whitman and Emerson, Merwin sees the poet as a representative man. He reasons that if *he* does not have the courage to stand up and fight for what he believes in, who will? The poet stands among partial men for the complete man, Emerson said. He should serve as a morally representative man, ready to sacrifice everything for the sake of his integrity and art.

On the other hand, poets must not dull their faculties in routine work. Merwin's epigraph for *A Mask for Janus* is: "Habit is evil, all habit, even speech / And promises prefigure their own breach." Life is a constant process of choosing what to do and be at the present moment. Habit must not be permitted to govern that choice. The truly free and original poet rejects the conventions of entangling relationships as well as the habitual clichés of speech. Just as one avoids the traps in human relationships, the poet tries to avoid the traps of conventional language.

Ironically, if speech is evil, as the critic Phillip Wheelwright maintains, then the epigraph is cast in the medium of evil, the currency of a fallen world. And promises, which must be communicated in speech, are contaminated by the medium, and hence they "prefigure their own breach."

The voice that emanates from the poetry of the first two volumes is the voice of a survivor recounting wonders in the wake of a transforming vision. The speaker in "When I Came from Colchis" in *The Dancing Bears* is perhaps most typical. He is a bard who has returned from the excursions to Colchis *and* Troy. He has captured the Golden Fleece and conquered Troy, yet he betrays a hesitancy about speaking of the wonders he has seen. This hesitancy may be born of fear of profaning them by setting them into words. He gallantly maintains that "the sunned / Sea" of his lady's eyes has robbed him of speech. Consequently, he can only relate his inability to articulate the mystery of the power of her presence. He asks, "What fable should I tell them, / That they should believe me?" (72)

The stasis of ripe, wordless perfection is captured in these almost dactylic lines from "You, Genoese Mariner." Merwin addresses Columbus:

> You, nevertheless, in search
> Of gilt and spice, who fancied
> Earth too circumscribed
> To imagine and cradle,
> Where no map had suspected
> The distance and marvels,
> The unfingered world—

> I . . . stand
> In the long light of wonder
> Staring upon shadows
> That circle and return
> From another's eyes,
> I, after so long,
> Who have been wrong as you. (F, 73)

The persona is that of an epic adventurer and voyager committed to his anabasis, his voyage in search of his own identity. Similarly, the young Merwin is questing and developing his identity as a poet. Perhaps Samuel Beckett has best expressed the spirit of his literary quest: "You must go on, you must say words, as long as there are any, until they find me, until they say me." As a gallant, dashing explorer, and experimenter in difficult verse forms, he has, like Byron or Yeats, learned his trade, learned the craft of verse; he finds and says the words he needs to say. Assured of certain modest immortality by the power of these words, he is capable of casting, as Yeats instructed, "a cold eye on life, on death."

The speaker of his poems, like the poet himself, is a man open to all possible loves and experiences. He is Janus-faced, looking constantly both toward the past and toward the future; correspondingly, the poetry is both traditional—grounded in myth and conventional verse forms—and prophetic. This latter capacity, nearly hidden in his early work, becomes more and more evident as Merwin comes to write poetry in open forms and as he begins to publish prose pieces with increasing frequency. The elegant, even chivalric voice remains essentially constant throughout the corpus of his work, though it becomes more intimate in *The Carrier of Ladders* and later books. This wanderer shares his anonymous origins and love of travel with the *picaro* Lazarillo de Tormes, whose tale Merwin later translated. The sensibility of the picaresque cavalier as well as his thirst for immortality, his openness to the poetic voyage of discovery, and his knowledge that belief is integral to the creative act are reflected in these lines from "Canso" in *The Dancing Bears:*

> Was there truly in that afternoon
> No sorcery, when the leaves between us
> In the October garden fell like words
> Through the long sun before gathering winter;
> Was there no enchantment but your imputation?

I was named inconstant; I had come
Unlooked for, from the shifting sea, my face
A field of doubting, my tales untrustworthy
You believed, and therewith I was credible. . . .

I am renewed as you imagine me
For all the orders love believes
Are the one order. (F, 108)

CHAPTER 2

Tracking the Animals and the Forgotten Language

> . . . I imagine
> A song not temporal wherein may walk
> The animals of time; I conceive a moment
> In which time and timelessness begin. (F, 118–119)
> "Canso," *The Dancing Bears*

I "The Perfect User of Words Uses Things"

DOMINATING Merwin's poetics in *A Mask for Janus* and *The Dancing Bears* is a compelling need to go beyond, into the unknown, in the domains of language and of experience and in reality itself. *A Mask for Janus* and *The Dancing Bears* were mythic quests for self-identity and for his own poetic voice. *Green with Beasts* is Merwin's declaration of identity and national origin. It is his book of Genesis, for in it, as in the Bible, Merwin undertakes the creation of the world, a world constructed of language and imagination, as well as the recreation of language.

Walt Whitman before Merwin believed that the value of poetry resides in the activity of language: Whitman asserted that meaning in poetry derives from an "activity of words rather than from any external significance attached to them." Moreover, "The perfect user of words uses things . . . Latent, in a great user of words, must actually be all passions, crimes, trades, animals, stars, God, sex, the past, might, space, metals and the like—because these are the words, and he who is not these, plays with a foreign tongue, turning helplessly to dictionaries and authorities."[1] The poet joins words to acts, words to things. Implicit in the lust for language is a lust for living and doing because words *are* things.

Emerson, whom both Whitman and Merwin read and revered, argued that if the word is infused with the vital essence of reality and is a symbol for the tangible object itself, then to push beyond the conventional, beyond established limits, and become an explorer in language is tantamount to pushing beyond—in life itself. Yet Emerson also wrote, "The invariable mark of wisdom is to see the miraculous in the common." Merwin undertakes both these tasks in *Green with Beasts*.

Linking his desire to portray beasts and saints—beasts *as* saints—and his search for a new language which will express the miraculous in the commonplace is a fundamentally religious impulse that Merwin channels into poetry and language. His motive is to capture and embody in the poem the impact of inspiration itself—be it religious or poetic. Language participates in this rite because it constructs and fixes the inner impact of inspiration or divine revelation verbally. Should language err, the element of the miraculous is lost; the poet has not earned the poem since the vision has not been recreated.

R. P. Blackmur, Merwin's mentor at Princeton, considers poetry an inspired manipulation of language:

Words, and their intimate arrangements, must be the ultimate as well as the immediate source of every effect in the written or spoken arts. Words bring meaning to birth and themselves contain the meaning as an imminent possibility before the pangs of junction. To the individual artist the use of words is an adventure in discovery; the imagination is heuristic among the words, it manipulates. The reality you labour desperately or luckily to put into your words . . . you will actually have found there, deeply ready and innately formed to give an objective being and specific idiom to what you know and did not know that you knew.[2]

In stressing the potential inherent in language and the poet's creative tapping of that potential, Blackmur is articulating one of Merwin's beliefs about poetry. The poet is both magus and artist, seeking the catalytic conversion of raw words into inspired meaning. The poet does not confine himself to a literal description of each separate object; instead he explores inward vistas, touching and tapping the meaning and truth latent in words before "the pangs of junction." The poetry produced is not rendered static by the fixity of concentration, the effort to express the impact of the object on the observer. On the contrary, Merwin's holy men, women, and animals in *Green with Beasts* are dynamic, experiencing consciousnesses. Consequently the reader participates in the unfolding of the poem itself; the poet leads him to observe, comment, question, puzzle out a situation for himself. The central consciousness of the poem—the subject—and the fascination with/in language share equal foci, each balanced against the other.

At this point a short digression in the form of a Biblical fable and exegesis may help to explain Merwin's choice of subject—animals—in *Green with Beasts*.

II   *The Holy Animals*

This is Merwin's parable for our time: After God created Adam and Eve, He instructed them to give names to the animals. He brought the animals to them one by one, and they were named. The names were magical in that they had rapport with the spiritual being of each animal, but unfortunately since then language has lost its original symbolic function. It, like man, fell. Call a wild animal by its name today. What happens?

What to make of a diminished thing? This is the basic existential, linguistic, and spiritual problem Merwin faces in his poetry. How to redeem language, to restore it to its original, symbolic "naming" function. The redemption of language is the poet's central task. The means of restoring it is through poetry. The poet's (impossible) aim is to find the names which will apply, or to invent the names to which the animals will respond, thereby reestablishing the unity of man and animal, man and nature, through language.

Unlike common human beings, beasts and saints seem never to have fallen from grace. They have, as one of Merwin's favorite poets Edwin Muir asserts, one foot in Eden. They retain some of the original radiance and as such are holier than human beings: they still walk in divine grace. They may even be capable of imparting some of their grace to human beings.

In 1969, Merwin published a chapbook of animal poems entitled *Animae*, Latin for "souls." For Merwin, animals *are* souls. Like *Animae*, *Green with Beasts* embodies a reverence for these creatures, even as it embodies a reverence for life. It is this, the same reverence and wonder "without which," W. H. Auden wrote in his Foreword to *A Mask for Janus*, "no man can become wise" (MJ, viii). As it succeeds in embodying awe and reverence, the poetry moves beyond the barriers of conventional linguistic statement, in the process giving new meaning to faded abstractions. For example, Mary speaks of her annunciation thus:

Though it itself it was like a word, and it was
Like no man and no word that ever was known,
Come where I was; and because I was nothing
It could be there. It was a word for
The way the light and the things in the light
Were looking into the darkness
And the things of the darkness were looking into the light
In the fullness, and the way the silence
Was hearing, like it was hearing a great song
And the song was hearing the silence forever
And forever and ever. (150)

The word she refers to is the *Logos,* the divine word made flesh. Only what Gerard Manley Hopkins calls the profound "inscape" of the annunciation is delineated here. The poet is certainly not intellectualizing the experience nor is he seeking to stratify, contain, or limit it. It retains its dynamism and mystery as a consequence of his re-creating it imagistically through the paradoxes of light and darkness, song and silence, fullness and nothingness. The description of the event is at the same time paradoxically spiritual and wholly physical. Mary's voice tentatively, tenderly ponders "the way of it in my heart, and how / The coming of it was a blessing" (151). In *Green with Beasts* he seeks through myth, religion, and poetry to reveal moments of the coming of the miraculous into the commonplace. He explores why and how it is that "God comes to see without a bell" (O, 279). If the treatment of subjects and events is from the outside in *A Mask for Janus* and *The Dancing Bears,* it is from the inside in *Green with Beasts.*

III   *After Babel and After the Deluge:*
The Animals from the Ark Walk Away

Angels and beasts resemble one another in that neither speaks because they have no need of speech. Being speech-blind or speech-free, they can never betray one another. They exist more easily in a preconscious state, the state in which Merwin writes his poetry.

Beasts, which Merwin regards as the very embodiment of the miraculous in the common, pose the problem of what is perceived, what is experienced when one has "no names to see with." They see and feel, yet having no words, they cannot tell what they see and feel. Like human beings, they can suffer terribly or experience peace, yet their inability to utter what they experience distinguishes their experience

radically from man's. In "White Goat, White Ram," Merwin recreates
the perceptions and experience of a goat, playing in the opening lines
on the apparent blindness of a goat whose eyes seem to focus off to the
sides of her but not together:

> So broadly is she blind
> Who has no names to see with: over her shoulder
> She sees not summer, not the idea of summer,
> But green meanings, shadows, the gold light of now, familiar
> The sense of long day-warmth, of sparse grass in the open
> Game of winds; an air that is plentitude,
> Describing itself in no name; all known before,
> Perceived many times before, yet not
> Remembered, or at most felt as usual. (F, 135)

Her blindness is no mere lack of sight: it derives from her being lan-
guage-blind, having "no names to see with," no words to apply to what
she is seeing or about to see, no mental constructs. Hence, "She sees
not summer, not the idea of summer," what humans mean by summer,
"But green meanings." The goat merely experiences the warmth and
air of the present moment, understands the green meaning of grass as
nourishment. She does not precisely remember this area "Perceived
many times before." At most, it is felt as usual. Merwin reasons that
goats have no cognitive memory: they cannot tell themselves that this
is where a certain event occurred last time or that this hillside looked
slightly different the summer before. To them, places simply seem
familiar or unfamiliar.

On the other hand, he believes animals have a strong moral faculty
and are capable of deciding between right and wrong. This faculty
becomes apparent as the goat becomes increasingly numinous under
his gaze. He realizes she has spiritual powers beyond human scope or
comprehension: " . . . and we go stricken suddenly / Humble, and the
covering of our feet / Offends, for the ground where we find we stand
is holy" (138).

Edwin Muir has a poem that is quite similar to this, which begins:
"They do not live in the world, / Are not in time and space / From
birth to death hurled / No word do they have, not one / To plant a
foot upon, / Were never in any place."[3] Muir's "The Animals," published in 1956, the same year as *Green with Beasts*, treats the same
themes as "White Goat, White Ram" and was quoted in its entirety by
Merwin in a long review of Muir's *Collected Poems* in the *New York*

Review of Books. Its final stanzas subsume the basic ideas of this chapter:

> For with names the world was called
> Out of empty air,
> With names was built and walled,
> Line and circle and square,
> Dust and emerald;
> Snatched from deceiving death
> By the articulate breath.
>
> But these have never trod
> Twice the familiar track,
> Never never turned back
> Into the memoried day.
> All is new and near
> In the unchanging Here
> On the fifth great day of God,
> That shall remain the same,
> Never shall pass away.
>
> On the sixth day we came.

In his review Merwin states that this poem is indicative of the "most striking theme in Muir's work." Then he makes a comment on Muir which applies equally well to his own poetry:

What I had failed to grasp earlier was the close and inevitable relation of the passage [to] the sum of Muir's work. The ambiguous power of the animals' presence in his writing is due in part to the fact that the world beyond time in which Muir's animals exist is at once the region from which man rose by virtue of his intelligence, and the Eden from which he fell and still falls. The animals also inhabit the fixed world of the fable, which in its chief details is the same for every life, yet is unique for each individual. It is becoming increasingly difficult, he believed, for modern man to distinguish its outlines, but the fable itself does not change.[4]

In the next to last sentence, Merwin is of course referring to the world of archetypes and of the collective unconscious. "The fable" is the unique story or account each creative individual makes of this world of archetypes—it is the manifestation of its movement and evolution within him. In Jungian psychology, "the fable" is seen as emanating

from the shadow or dream existence. In a revealing note to Paul Carroll on the animal in "Words from a Totem Animal" and the wolf-
spirit in "Lemuel's Blessing," Merwin explains that the animals in
many of his poems are similar to heraldic animals: "These animals are
not chosen and refuse to be identified, absolutely, zoologically. They
rise, as it were, from dreams, facing away, and no more want that kind
of partial identification than the Other wishes to divulge a name."[5] By
"the Other" Merwin means the transcendent power whose engagement he perceives when a poem is initiated.

Despite his proud gift of speech and naming, man lives in the
"empty air" outside the Eden that the animals and angels inhabit. Muir
says the animals were called "out of empty air," and Merwin, that they
live in a "world beyond time," the paradise on earth from which man
"fell and still falls." It would seem that for Merwin the poet's effort is
to stop this inevitable process of reversion. There may even be the res-
idue of some very primitive beast worship in the lines of both poets, an
atavistic yearning for the simplicity and innocence of the animals'
knowledge, a nostalgia for the time when man still had "one foot in
Eden."

When Muir declares, "For with names the world was called . . .
With names was built and walled, / Line and circle and square" he
reflects an aesthetic tenet shared by Emerson, Whitman, Mallarmé,
and Rimbaud as well as Merwin: he affirms that language fixes and
builds nonverbal as well as verbal reality, physical as well as aesthetic
reality. And Muir's image of the poet's physical crafting of the world
is reminiscent of similar images Urizen uses in Blake's *Jerusalem*.

In "Dictum: For a Masque of Deluge" Merwin describes an event
near the day of creation, though not at the actual time of creation. The
occasion is after the Flood, when the ark has been emptied:

> . . . the beasts depart; the man
> Whose shocked speech must conjure a landscape
> As of some country where the dead years keep
> A circle of silence, a drying vista of ruin,
> Musters himself, rises, and stumbling after
> The dwindling beasts, under the all-colored
> Paper rainbow, whose arc he sees as promise,
> Moves in amazement of resurrection,
> Solitary, impoverished, renewed, (F, 40)

Throughout the entire poem up to this point the words have been lik-
ened to rain, and silence to dryness. The "masque" is the noisy patter

of rain "like a blather of words." During the masque, the beasts are led into the ark. When the Flood subsides, they depart, abandoning man, whose first impulse is to follow them and implore their help. Catching himself, however, he stands looking after them "under the all-colored / Paper rainbow," that is blatantly artificial, fooling only man. In lines heavy with irony Merwin portrays the man moving away "in an amazement of resurrection, / Solitary, impoverished, renewed." The passage seems ambiguous at first, containing its stark contrast between desolation and satisfaction. Man believes he is resurrected when in fact he is impoverished by the beasts' departure.

In these lines we perceive the animals' relevance to Merwin's conception of language: man had hoped that he and the animals together would be fellow-builders of the world. But having no language, the animals must walk away from his world-building, they cannot remain to aid him in conjuring a landscape. Ironically, they fade into a landscape *he* had conjured and created with his words. They pass under his "Paper rainbow," God's promise of resurrection to man, *not* to the beasts. Language—and apparently God—cleave a gulf between the beasts and man. Though they move into the world man has built with his names, they move beyond time in "the fixed world of heraldic symbols," and the world of fable and of the unconscious. Human guilt about animals derives from this fact: the beasts were man's original valued companions, fellow inhabitants of the newly created earth, partners in wonder. God separates these original equals by commanding man to name the beasts. Names and words are of uncertain value: they force human beings ultimately to find, as Merwin says in the last stanza of "Dictum: For a Masque of Deluge": "Dictions for rising, words for departure." Words or "Dictions" become the emblems of our separation from the rest of animate nature.[6] Man can achieve definite immortality through words; animals seldom do. On the other hand, Merwin wrote in "Canso" of the animals' timeless mode of existence as heraldic animals: "I imagine / A song not temporal wherein may walk / The animals of time; I conceive a moment / In which time and that timelessness begin" (F, 118–119). Animals are always imagined as creatures who inhabit a realm where time and the eternal meet.

IV   Animae *(1969)*

A decade ago and well over a decade after *Green with Beasts* was published in 1956, Merwin brought out *Animae*, which plays on the child's pronunciation of "animals" and is the plural for the Latin word *soul*.

The last poem of the ten-poem sequence which includes "Lemuel's Blessing" borrows Muir's title "The Animals" and shares the post-Deluge mood of "Dictum: For a Masque of Deluge":

> All these years behind windows
> With blind crosses sweeping the tables
> And myself tracking over empty ground
> Animals I never saw
>
> I with no voice
>
> Remembering names to invent for them
> Will any come back will one
> Saying yes
> Saying look carefully yes
> We will meet again. (L, 3)

The opening image has multiple associations: the first line indicates separation; and when combined with the second line, it produces a cinematic impression of the passage of time. The tables may symbolize the speaker's own life, the blind crosses, symbols of the God who separated man and the animals to begin with. The blind crosses could be interpreted as symbols of the religion which cannot see and will not save him. Human salvation or affirmation, when it comes, must come from the animals, hence the search for them—"myself tracking over empty ground." Here "empty ground" recalls Muir's phrase "empty air" and Merwin's "drying vista of ruin" from "Dictum: For a Masque of Deluge."

Ironically, though the poet like the animals has no voice, still he must "invent names for them." Has God commanded it? The poet meditates and questions, "Will any come back will one / Saying yes / Saying look carefully yes / We will meet again." Here the poem progresses toward a confrontation with an unseen animal that the poet has called back. It also may anticipate yet another meeting—in another life? The encounter with the animals would manifest the validity of his invented names; it would create the possibility of *his* saying "yes" and validate his trust in the attainment of unity between animals and man. In addition, the achieved "we" in the final line would necessitate an acceptance of "myself" by the animal.

Implicit in "The Animals" is the redemption of language. Words—in this case "yes"—would finally be used for a caring, constructive, positive purpose. Rather than merely fabricating presences out of emptiness, words would be used to express love and community. Those who meet Merwin are impressed by the stark contrast between his own personal warmth and the cool impersonality of his poems. If language ceased to be effective in the expression of passion or love after the Deluge, if Babel then ensued, dividing mankind by making people incapable of communicating in the same language, what can the poet do but learn the language of silence? In "Whenever I Go There," the speaker says, "I go my way eating the silence of animals." The poet can only issue messages from the silence at the core of being.

He sees animals as sacrifices to technology: they are no longer man's companions at the plough, sharing intimately in his everyday life as they did in the nineteenth century. In his review of Edwin Muir's work, Merwin quotes this illuminating passage from Muir's *Autobiography:*

> My passion for animals comes partly from being brought up close to them ... partly from I know not where. Two hundred years ago the majority of people lived close to the animals by whose labor or flesh they existed. The fact that we live on these animals remains; but the personal relation is gone, and with it the very ideas of necessity and guilt. ... A rationalist would smile at the thought that there is any guilt at all: there is only necessity, he would say. ... I do not know whether many people have dreams of animals. ... But it is certain that people who have been brought up in close contact with animals, including the vast majority of the generations from whom we spring, have dreamed and dream of animals, and my own experience shows that these dreams are often tinged with a guilt of which consciously we are unaware.[7]

Along with Muir, Merwin feels guilt when he contemplates animals. In his poetry he acknowledges their sensitivity and keen senses and knows that they are justified in abandoning man since man has abandoned them in at least two major ways: first, he adopted world-making speech, which created a gap between humans and animals, and then he shunted them aside in favor of machines. No longer working with animals in the fields, man lost his former awareness of their inner lives. Consequently, they become all the more anonymous to him and merge with his dream animals. The dream creatures intrigue both Merwin and Muir since they appear to be visitors from the other world, the

world of the unconscious. In the dreamlike creative state, the symbol-
and name-making mind engages what Merwin calls "the Other," the
source of creativity itself. Then the animals emerge from their solitary
vigil in the "empty ground" of the unconscious.

At these moments of welling creativity and illumination, Merwin
experiences pure freedom: "Then there is the 'freedom' that accompanies poetry at a distance and occasionally joins it, often without
being recognized" (NP, 279). The moment of creativity approaches
sacred experience for him. He experiences the coalescing of a poem as
a kind of divine visitation. In Merwin's thought the guilt Muir men-
tions is transformed into a desire for reunification with the animals. He
longs to strengthen his bonds with them.

V   *Joining the Sacred Wolves*

In "The Paw," Merwin imagines a reunion with an animal soulmate
occurring simultaneously with a reunion with his own body:

> I return to my limbs with the first
> gray light
> and here is the gray paw under my hand
> the she-wolf Perdita
> has come back
> to sleep beside me
> her spine pressed knuckle to knuckle
> down my front
> her ears lying against my ribs
> on the left side where the heart beats (CL, 119)

The speaker merges physically with the wolf's body—"gray paw
under my hand, / her spine pressed knuckle to knuckle / down my
front." Later in the poem he imagines racing with the wolf, whose
name means "The Lost One" in Latin: "racing over the dark auroras
/ you and I with no shadow." The two metamorphose into pure spirits,
travelling fleetly, hastening toward an apocalyptic consummation reminiscent of that described in Rimbaud's "Aube":

> I beat faster
> her blood wells through my fingers
> my eyes shut to see her
> again
> my way

> before the stars fall
> and the mountains go out
> and void wakes
> and it is day
>
> but we are gone

As he comes to inhabit her body, he becomes the wolf herself at the moment before each vanishes. The swift movement of this poem and its breathless cadences make it difficult to decipher whether or not she is actually alive or dead in these final lines. If dead, she lives on physically in his self. The two have merged in spirit: they pass away together in death and the void in the sentence "but we are gone." As quickly as the vision came, the empty ground of "the void wakes" to supplant it. Even the natural cycles are reversed at the instant of mystic consummation—"the mountains go out" and "the stars fall." Man falls once more from his Eden where he was in communion with his God. As the speaker loses the immediacy of this pure contact, he loses his very existence, too.

To the extent that they are keys to the human soul and the life beyond, animals resemble gods in Merwin's poetry. Certainly they precipitate moments of sacred consummation, as in "The Paw," or revelation, as in "White Goat, White Ram," or "Dog." They exist in a dream reality between waking and sleeping. They live in a time when "All is new and near / In the unchanging Here / On the fifth great day of God."

It is interesting to observe that in "The Paw" the consummation with the Other, the she-wolf, necessitates such a great selflessness that the speaker actually moves from his own body into hers so that "her blood wells through my fingers." Likewise in *Green with Beasts* in "The Annunciation" Mary experiences the same selflessness during the immanence of the annunciation:

> . . . Only, in the place
> Where, myself, I was nothing, there was suddenly
> A great burning under the darkness, a fire
> Like fighting up into the wings' lash and the beating
> Blackness, and flames like the tearing of teeth,
> With noise like rocks rending, such that no word
> Can call it as it was there. (149)

During the creative act or divine union, there is complete selflessness, "myself, I was nothing." Instead the spiritual plane of existence subsumes all other planes. When the moment of union is past, "no word / Can call it as it was there," but Merwin counsels in "Learning a Dead Language," "What you remember saves you."

"Lemuel's Blessing" from *Animae* is another poem that treats wolves in relation to the sacred. Throughout, Lemuel is invoking a "Spirit," possibly a wolf-spirit or totem animal spirit. Lemuel himself is the sort of animal Merwin describes in his letter, the kind that rises "from dreams, facing away, and no more want that kind of partial identification than the Other wishes to divulge a name."[8]

Lemuel is making a prayer to the "Spirit." In so doing, he recalls other Lemuels of sacred and religious literature. He has rapport with both King Lemuel of the Hebrews (Proverbs 31:1–31) and the Lemuel of Christopher Smart's *Jubilate Agno:* the latter is the subject of the poem's epigraph. That epigraph provides a point of vital ingress into the poem, which itself is cast in the form of a Hebrew psalm of lament.

The Lemuel of Proverbs learns certain lessons from his mother, who counsels him against lust, drinking, and other sins of intemperance, sins which would undermine his ability to govern effectively. Addressing this Lemuel, Smart exhorts him to "Bless with the wolf, which is a dog without a master, but the Lord hears his cries and feeds him in the desert. (AN, 11). Finally, in his elliptical fashion, Merwin creates a Lemuel who *is* the wolf who begs his Spirit to give him purity and strength in his independence and solitary exile. He asks to be preserved "From the ruth of the lair," "the ruth of kindness, with its licked hands," "the ruth of approval," "the ruth of known paths." The tone is both bitter and worshipful. The lines open like highways into the desert; and his "From the ruth of . . ." and "Preserve" repetitions provide a psalmic structuring device. The speaker humbles himself before the Spirit: "I am nothing but a dog lost and hungry." By the time of *The Carrier of Ladders,* roughly seven years later, Merwin would have broken the line after "nothing," but here the lines have a prosy length and muscle. The wolf's *raison d'être* appears to be running, and there is a fine image of the sound of running in a section in which he foresees his taking refuge: "Another time, if I need it, / Create a little wind like a cold finger between my shoulders, then / Let my nails pour out a torrent of aces like grain from a threshing machine" (AN, 13).

Even to a greater extent than the fox of "Plea for a Captive" in *The Drunk in the Furnace,* this animal is highly conscious of his moral position concerning the lures of civilization. He has not had the moral energy tamed out of him and will not indulge in the comforts of civilization. He resists the blandishments of flatterers and the temptation to seek refuge in a secure income and snug berth. In this he is a wolf who voices Merwin's own moral imperative of freedom. In his personal life the poet always has chosen to reject the security of the fixed associations and the comfortable niche of a university teaching job or an editorship. Instead he has retained total freedom, living without permanent dependents or any guarantee of a permanent income. He is free to depart for France or Mexico at a moment's notice, just as he is free, like the wolf, to die alone in the desert.

Lemuel's request for his "cry" echoes Merwin's wish for his own poems and prose:

> But let me leave my cry stretched out behind me like a road
> On which I have followed you.
> And sustain me for my time in the desert
> On what is essential to me. (A, 13)

Merwin's counsel to the reader in "For Now" is: "Tell me what you see vanishing and I / Will tell you who you are" (MT, 93). Yet what he sees vanishing is poignantly obvious in the foregoing poems, and it is treated in a question-and-answer poem from *The Lice* where an unnamed speaker queries what man's hands are doing: "No what are the hands / A. Climbing back down the museum wall / To their ancestors the extinct shrews that will / Have left a message" (L, 6).

VI   *Merwin's Genesis*

> Canst thou draw out Leviathan with an
> hook? or his tongue with a cord which thou
> lettest down? (Job 4:1)

Well schooled in the Biblical creation story as a child, Merwin is aware that after making the firmament and the earth, light and darkness, the sun and the moon, God made the animals. The first created of all creatures are the "great whales," hence "Leviathan" is set first in the bestiary opening *Green with Beasts*. And since birds were created next, the "Blue Cockerel" is second.

"Leviathan," in its primitive energy and imaginative reach, echoes

Pound's "Seafarer" and before that early English poetry. The emphasis
is on a return to sources—here the Anglo-Saxon. And once again, the
emphasis is on naming: "He is called Leviathan, and named for rolling
/ First created was he of all creatures, / He has held Jonah three days
and nights / He is that curling serpent that in ocean is" (127).

This poem is more objective, concrete, definite, and declarative than
any in his two earlier books. Substance and metaphysical meaning
intertwine: "Sea-fright he is." Paradoxically, through narrowing his
topic the poet has broadened his range. His focus is on the essentials.
These lines stand stark and solid against the backdrop of the glittering,
tense verbal constructs of the more sophisticated earlier poetry. If the
former poems described events or experiences, this poem *presents* the
experience of Leviathan himself. An ebullient exaltation in the abilities
of language to invoke the metaphysical reality of the serpent carries
the poem forth simply on its own momentum. The rolling, choppy
rhythms capture the rolling and wet slapping of the creature.

Basic declarative statement, surprise at ontological discovery,
pounding meter converge to re-create the wonder and reverence felt
by the Anglo-Saxons and their bards as they witnessed the movements
of Leviathan. An effective stylistic technique is Merwin's use of Anglo-
Saxon kennings, crystallized poems in themselves, "Shoulders spouting,
the fist of his forehead." These two-part lines, divided alliteratively,
reflect a primitive, joyous poetic consciousness. The poem's final lines
affirm primordiality in their explosion of alliteratively hooked words
reminiscent of Gerard Manley Hopkins: "Star-climbed, wind-combed,
cumbered with itself still / As at first it was, is the hand not yet contented / Of the creator. And he waits for the world to begin" (128).

In writing a poem which sends down roots into Anglo-Saxon literature rather than into the Classical Greek mythology that inspired his
other books, Merwin is himself beginning the world again. *He* is the
Creator "not yet contented," *he* "subdues" the world through descrip-
tions of it and its monsters of the deep. The time is the beginning of
time, the place, his newly created world, his genesis.

Next comes the creation of the birds. It is fitting that the blue cockerel of the next poem should have "one eye / Glaring like the sun's self
(for there is no other). / Like the sun seen small, seen rimmed in red
secret" (129). God made "the lights of the firmament," sun and moon,
on the fourth day of creation, while He made birds on the fifth.

After making the whales, sea monsters, and fish, God made "the
beasts of the earth after his kind, and cattle after their kind, and every

thing that creepeth upon the earth after his kind" (Genesis 1:25); therefore "Two Horses," "Dog," and "White Goat, White Ram" ensue.
Even though they are familiar domestic animals, they are seen by Merwin as imbued with potent otherworldly power and, in the case of the
dog, with danger.

The sea's self partakes of the life of the horses:

> And these horses stamp
> Before us now in this garden; and northward
> Beyond the terraces the misted sea
> Swirls endless, hooves of the gray wind forever
> Thundering, churning the ragged spume-dusk . . .
> Porpoises plunging like the necks of horses. (132)

In greek myth Poseidon is sometimes conceived of as being part man,
part porpoise, holding a trident. These sea horses, waves curling
mightily and then crashing onto the shore, recall those of Matthew
Arnold, in "The Forsaken Merman": "Now the wild white horses play
/ Champ and chafe and toss in the spray." Likewise the line from
"Leviathan," "Heavily, his wake hoary behind him" (127), evokes Job
41:32, which proclaims, "He maketh a path to shine after him; one
would think the deep to be hoary." In the poem "Two Horses," what
are familiar, reliable domestic animals become exotic sea creatures,
uncontained and uncontainable.

Similarly, in the next poem "Dog" the animal's gaze startles the
speaker with its ghostly, unreal object: "Look again: it is through you
/ That he looks, and the danger of his eyes / Is that in them you are
not there. He guards indeed / What is gone, what is gone" (134). As
in "The Paw" where "the void wakes" and swallows speaker and she-
wolf, here the danger is that "you" (the reader) will be swallowed up
in what the dog guards. Just like "the shimmering vista of emptiness"
where the dog dwells, the persistent subject and theme of "Dog," the
poem itself is singularly static; it treats the dog's, the speaker's, and the
reader's relation to the void. But what is unusual here is that the
speaker is constantly instructing "you," the reader, seriously and a bit
self-righteously, warning him how to avoid falling prey to the dog's
spiritual vacancy, an absence which overtakes the soul:

> Walk past him
> If you please, unmolested, but behind his eyes

You will be seen not to be there, in the glaring
Uncharactered reaches of oblivion, and guarded
With the rest of vacancy. Better turn from him
Now when you can and pray that the dust you stand in
And your other darlings be delivered
From the vain distance he is the power of. (134)

The reference to "your other darlings" seems unnecessarily pompous
as well as rather dated today. And "uncharactered reaches" is a curious
description of oblivion, implying as it does that any charactered or
written-on expanse is to some extent part of the known world. But
despite its supercilious tone, the poem's agony and despair at confronting this being (or nothingness?) guarding "the rest of vacancy" recall
the despair and futility of T. S. Eliot's *The Waste Land*. If one thinks
of *The Waste Land* as the preparation for Eliot's religious conversion,
the experience of "Dog" is the reverse of a religious conversion; I
would, however, venture that the same might be said of *The Waste
Land*, too. In "Dog," instead of being ushered into a knowledge of the
fullness of God, the reader is made aware of the emptiness of this being
who emobdies the power of "vain distance." This distance may be the
expanse of Hades, the underworld, and the dog may be Cerberus, its
guardian. Or on a more intimate level, distance may represent the hell
of the self in too deep myopic introspection. Whatever it is, certainly
this dog has strong symbolic meaning. In his Genesis in *Green with
Beasts* and his description of the animals inhabiting "the desert of the
unknown" in *Animae*, Merwin has collected and named certain animals one by one so that in the end no one—and no word—would be
lost.

VII   *Whole Earth Epilogue*

In his later poems published after *Green with Beasts*, from the early
1960s on, Merwin's animals are not merely the passive recipients of
man's attentions. They are not simply representations of "the miraculous in the common," they come to symbolize the voice of the wilderness talking back to man, for as Thoreau asserted, "In wildness is the
preservation of the world."

Like Lemuel, the animals of the later poems rebuke man indirectly
or ironically for his moral degeneracy. The poem addressed to the gray
whale in "For a Coming Extinction" powerfully, if indirectly, casts

shame on the whale's human predators for their ecological destructiveness. All the later animal poems deal in one way or another with the grasping greed and predatoriness of human nature as opposed to the innocent flight of the beasts. Their focus is on man's inhumanity to animals. One can observe a measure of Romanticism here—a validation of the good in wild nature and the evil in the ways of the civilized—but the polarity has a direct correspondence to the actuality of modern man's despoiling, polluting, and otherwise using wild nature only for his own purposes, with no thought given to the morality of what he is doing. Out of self-defense, Merwin's recent animals, if they are not extinct, have teeth, nails, and claws—and know how to use them. There are ravens, everywhere regarded as prophets of woe, coyotes, wolves, and foxes.

These animals and animal spirits consciously elude humans. They are aware that "the names" we make for them do not apply and would "fit anything." In "Words for a Totem Animal," published in 1970, in *The Carrier of Ladders*, the totem animal, an animal spirit to whom humans, probably Indians, pray, discusses its plight:

> Caught again and held again
> again I am not a blessing
> they bring me
> names
> that would fit anything
> they bring them to me
> they bring me hopes
> all day I turn
> making ropes
> helping (CL, 16)

The irony of his situation is emphasized by the irrational linking through rhyme of "hopes" and "ropes." Instead of fulfilling hopes he can only make ropes, but perhaps they, like the ladder in the title *The Carrier of Ladders*, are vehicles for ascending.

The inapplicability of the fallen names humans give him is only one sign of the animal's inaccessibility and essential mystery. It would seem, as the poem progresses, that no names fit aspects of nature anymore: "there are no names for rivers / for the day for the nights" which vanish without trace, so there is no longer any possibility of naming them. The totem animal, however, *can* remember "how it was

/ with one foot in a name" (CL, 17). And even the totem animal appears to be seeking his own inner unity:

> My eyes are waiting for me
> in the dusk
> they are still closed
> they have been waiting for a long time
> and I am feeling my way toward them . . .
> Maybe I will come
> to where I am one
> and find
> I have been waiting there
> as a new
> year finds the song of the nuthatch (CL, 16, 19)

Isn't unity what the poet himself is seeking? Will the two seekers ever converge? Perhaps.

We have seen how Merwin justifies the wild and familiar animals and the totem animals, proclaiming in all his poems their right to exist free, unhampered, unhunted, or unhaunted by humans. Beyond this, Merwin also sees a relationship between wild and tame animals on the one hand, and the private and public spheres of *human* existence on the other. The wild animals exemplify the purest (human) integrity whereas the domesticated animals seem slavishly content to wallow in the luxury of their provided food and lodging. "Fly" from *Animae* embodies Merwin's feelings of repulsion for a tame pigeon: "I have been cruel to a fat pigeon / Because he would not fly / . . . He had let himself become a wreck filthy and confiding / . . . beating the cat off the garbage." The poet repeatedly throws him into the air, trying to force him to fly, but to no avail. Later he finds him "in the dovecote dead / Of the needless efforts." Well aware of his own culpability, the poet ponders the pigeon's "eye that could not / Conceive that I was a creature to run from / I who have always believed too much in words" (AN, 25).

Merwin has a far greater respect for any creature who would willingly commit suicide or flee than serve or be enslaved. He has lost respect for the American people for the same reasons: they have been indoctrinated and "tamed" by their government. They passively accept the loss of their freedom while "silence the climber falls from the cliffs" (CL, 57). In the poem "Presidents" where the "president of lies" figures prominently, it is significant that "the cliffs," the wilderness, are the sole refuge of what the people express—"silence." Wild, rugged nature is the haven of truth and of the free, those who would escape confrontation with sustained political deceit and live untainted by American political actuality. Only in the wilderness can one "Avoid News by the River," and absorb the innocence, strength, and well-being of the ravens and wolves.

Merwin sees a profound split between the physical and the spiritual in America today. The body of the American people, the body politic, has become defiled, hence the spiritual wreaks its ghostly vengeance from the outreaches of desert and forest. The poem from *The Carrier of Ladders*, "The Free" is spoken by these ghostly voices:

> So far from the murders
> the ruts begin to bleed
> but no one hears
> our voices
> and the sound of the reddening feet
> they leave us the empty roads
> they leave us . . .
> and when we have gone they say we are forever (CL, 58)

These lines could have been spoken by any of the extinct species. And Merwin's strong sympathy with the dead seems justified when one consults any list of the extinct and soon-to-be-extinct animals. Our world's ecological balance has also been irretrievably disrupted by our greed, pollution, and profiteering. Communion with the animals, admission into an intimacy with them, would only be possible were man a creative rather than a destructive master of his environment. He might even become merely a cohabitant of the earth, sharing it with the animals rather than mastering it, as Gary Snyder has suggested. In Merwin's eyes the true beasts are the human beings, who are luxury-addicted, materialistic pigeons. Though man is obviously technologically and, for the most part, intellectually superior to the animals, they are wiser. Our long domination over them has corrupted us, making us more bestial than they. *King Lear* clearly reveals such a regression: Lear loses his highest human faculties and sinks to a state lower than the bestial. When humans become dehumanized, lose their ethical frame of reference, animals appear to have better developed faculties of moral discrimination. And truly, "In wildness is the salvation of the world."

At their best the animals of all Merwin's poems can be conceived of as teachers—even teachers of and "speakers of the word for heaven." In this capacity, they teach man through example since they are his rightful original companions. The word, though now after Babel an inadequate, fallen vehicle of communication, remains our only means of communication with the animals. In using it correctly lies our salvation because, despite man's atrocities, when he has successfully remembered "names to invent for them," communication will be effected: one will come back "Saying yes saying look carefully yes / We will meet again." Language and the world—the human and animal worlds—will be redeemed.

In *After Babel*, George Steiner states: "The Kabbalah, in which the problem . . . of the nature of language is so insistently examined, knows of a day of redemption on which . . . All human tongues will have re-entered the translucent immediacy of that primal, lost speech shared by God and Adam.[9] Merwin speculates that it is shared and understood by the animals, as well. Curiously, animals have been saving us all along with their voices. In a brief poem from *Animae*, he says:

At midsummer before dawn an orange light returns to the mountains
Like a great weight and the small birds cry out
And bear it up.

The poem is called "How We Are Spared."

CHAPTER 3

Descendants

It seems that only now
We realize the depth of the water, the
Abyss over which we float among such
Clouds.
W. S. Merwin, "The Iceberg"

I The Release into Mortality

THE sea poems of *The Drunk in the Furnace* (1960) trace the
poet's awakening to new knowledge and a new conception of
objective experience. The poems show the mind's journey from first
impressions through perceptions to understanding. Recognition attends
each sea poem's ending. The last lines are beginnings: they are the
prodigal son's first steps toward home. It is the moment of decision and
revelation that attracts Merwin. While "Leviathan" and other poems
from the bestiary of *Green with Beasts* expressed "the emblematic
presentment of the world's fierce energies,"[1] these poems of *The
Drunk in the Furnace* betray extreme personal commitment and close
tracking of the inner psychological path toward revelation. Richard
Howard finds here "the desperate calcination of a man in a death
struggle . . . with his own *realization,* in all the senses that word will
bear, of mortality."[2]

Death is the unknowable, both sought and fled. In the first two
books, the tightly crafted forms and meters are erected as bulwarks
against the incursions of mortality. Alice Benston discusses the
speaker's stance thus: "The speaker, whose condition is death, has no
sympathy with doctrines of promised future resurrection or the idea
that a life exists despite the loss of his love."[3] Before, the poet's whole
aim was to ensure both the relationship and the poetry itself against
the possible erosions of mortality:

There must be found, then, the imagination
Before the names of things, the dicta for

> The only poem, and among all dictions
> That ceremony whereby you may be named
> Perpetual out of the anonymity
> Of death. (F, 114)

Finding that ceremony—either in poetry or in other spheres of existence—has proved impossible. But at the moment of his release into mortality the poet evinces, instead of despair, only a recognition of his own deepening knowledge of self and of his own true poetic voice. Karl Malkoff discusses the technical side of this liberation of form and content: "Once a poet of intricate pattern, Merwin now uses free verse almost exclusively; the syntax is frequently fragmented, the language is less precious, less archaic, and much tougher."[4] He writes in a tenser, plainer, more colloquial idiom, one first adopted in "The Annunciation." It is as though he were picking up the simple language of his ancestors, the seamen and Yankee natives of the Eastern seaboard whom he embodies in *The Drunk in the Furnace*. One of the voices might be that of his grandfather the Allegheny river pilot.[5] Merwin objectively records the real details of any given scene as well as the musings that lead to the speaker's growing awareness of reality. As in *Green with Beasts* the poems are narratives. In Richard Howard's assessment, they are "ruminations or arguments, affording what [the poet] Miss [Marianne] Moore calls 'a gallantry of observation' rather than the exuberance of design—they are not prose, but they have some of the virtues of prose, for they are able to accommodate the ordinary sights and sounds of life without transforming them into myth."[6] If *Green with Beasts* was his Genesis, this is his Job, celebrating the awesome power of the sea and of the unknown. Or, on a more pedestrian level, it is his Book of Numbers, listing the members of his tribe.

Reversal and recognition are the central dramatic techniques employed in *The Drunk in the Furnace*. Merwin's ironic effects stem from the shock of reversal and recognition. But the recognition is a recognition of the power wielded by mysterious forces beyond human control. Certainly his background as a dramatist is as apparent here in his choice of techniques as it was in his casting "Dictum: For a Masque of Deluge" in the genre of "stage directions."[7] Behind each of the sea poems is the gloating face of the Greek tragedian who tips the tables— or boats—on an expectant but presumably complacent audience. The scenario of each sea poem is the same: the speaker ventures out to sea, and the reader and speaker are initiated into the sea's mysteries. The sunny sailing voyage ends in disaster; bad weather descends, a violent storm sinks ships. A familiar face is seen distorted in grimace. Or worse, the face of one dead haunts the wondering speaker so that what he had understood to be a routine voyage changes his life, putting "All of disaster between us: a gulf / Beyond reckoning. It begins where we are." (F, 210) Enjambment and strong central caesuras, both of which emphasize recognitions by dislocating natural line rhythms, operate to disrupt established concepts and disassociate ordinary perception. These strong poetic cues are necessary, Merwin believes, because we tend to take the familiar so much for granted. Is landscape "deceiving / By seeming familiar, but an image merely / By which one may know the face of emptiness, / A name with which to say emptiness?" (F, 143)

Newness breeds wonder, awe. On the other side of that seemingly calm landscape or seascape dwell mystery and emptiness, the void of death. When our eyes are opened wide to the mystery, "A terrible beauty is born." These gothic poems begin in deceptive calm, even occasionally in gaiety, only to spiral in deeper and deeper arcs of philosophical speculation. Ultimately, the speaker confronts a deeper level of metaphysical or supernatural awareness, what Merwin has called "the Other,"[8] what Rainer Maria Rilke called "the Angel." Each poem is a withering into truth. The reader comes away feeling an emotion that is best expressed in his line from *The Carrier of Ladders*, "Strange / to be any place" (CL, 116). Here "The invariable mark of wisdom" is not "the miraculous in the common," but the *mysterious* in the common—the existence of profound mystery in the common.

II   *The Void of Ocean*

Ocean is one of the voids in *The Drunk in the Furnace*. According to Richard Howard, here Merwin is concerned with "the sea, its never-ending finality, its irreversible otherness 'beyond reckoning' of which he remarks, in *Favor Island*, 'there's only one side to the ocean, and nothing on the other . . . and always there is the noise, making a kind of silence in which nothing can be heard.'"[9] Speech without meaning is the mad song of the sea. Like the Other, the sea is unfathomable. It is the proper habitation for those who forge their own destinies, as "Noah's Raven" defiantly attests:

> I found untouched the desert of the unknown,
> Big enough for my feet. It is my home.
> It is always beyond them. The future

Splits the present with the echo of my voice.
Hoarse with fulfillment, I never made promises. (AN, 7)

The sea, itself a "desert of the unknown," has a murderous innocence. In Merwin's poetry the sea is the fearful, ominous sea of *Moby
Dick* and of Melville's poetry. If no I. A. Coffin figures sardonically
here as in *Moby Dick*, still there is a definite presumption of the sea's
deceptiveness. Various poems reveal the irony of our entrusting ourselves to the sea on a clear morning. In Merwin's poetry, as in Melville's, the sea is emblematic of a whole philosophy of life. The sea, like
life itself, is not as it appears on the surface: it harbors monsters in its
depths, "a darkness under / The surface, between us and the land,
twisting." (F, 211) This darkness moves between us and the land, pre-
venting our retreat. Like Melville, Merwin—a Navy man and a
descendant of a river pilot—knows that any navigator who is not constantly alert to the protean changes of the sea is a fool.

Land at least can be measured and marked by fences and boundaries. Some degree of limitation, of human ordering, is possible
although, significantly, in his poems focusing on the land, Merwin
often treats the bizarre or unexpected events which occur on land:
floods are a favorite preoccupation (F, 172), and so are "holy" mountains (F, 154–7, 252–5). But in "Low Fields and Light" he presents the
image of fields and fences running into the sea:

The flat fields run out to the sea there.
There is no sand, no line. It is autumn.
The bare fields, dark between fences, run
Out to the idle gleam of the flat water.
And the fences go on out, sinking slowly,
With a cow-bird half-way . . . watching
How the light slides through them easy as weeds
Or wind, slides over them away out near the sky
Because even a bird can remember
The fields that were there before the slow
Spread and wash of the edging light crawled
There and covered them, a little more each year. (F, 184)

Here the ocean, like light, flows over boundaries civilization has tried
to set up between one man's property and another's. When one thinks
of fencing off sections of the sea, the idea of owning the sea begins to

seem absurd. Correspondingly, on a technical level, the poem's rhythmic flow disrupts the boundaries of the line through enjambment. Lines flow over into each other as light, weeds, or wind flow past or run over fences.

An iceberg—a frozen portion of the sea—is an appropriate symbol for the distance, hostile cold, and silence of the sea. In wondering tones, the speaker of Merwin's poem "The Iceberg" stumbles upon the mystery, the silence of life:

> It seems that only now
> We realize the depth of the waters, the
> Abyss over which we float among such
> Clouds. And still not understanding
> The coldness of most elegance, even
> With so vast and heartless a splendor
> Before us, stare, caught in the magnetism
> Of great silence, thinking: this is the terror
> That cannot be charted, this is only
> A little of it. (F, 202)

The linebreaks between "the / Abyss" and "such / Clouds" force a reader to pause between lines; they give a hesitancy to the metaphorical naming of ocean and iceberg. The act of seeing into the mystery of life necessitates a guardedness since in seeing deeply one confronts and viscerally experiences "the terror / That cannot be charted, this is only / A little of it." Of this unchartable terror Professor Gary Thompson writes, "He notes its existence and location on the map, but he seems incapable of exploring it. In other words, he defines the perimeters of the mysterious. Merwin's problem at this point seems to be a yearning to go down and explore the abyss, but he is incapable of doing so."[10] He can only "stand and learn," filled with awe. This act of wondering realization is repeated over and over in the sea poems of *The Drunk in the Furnace*.

In "The *Portland* Going Out," a poem which tells of the departure of the *Portland* which was to sink off Cape Cod on November 26, 1898, an intimacy with calamity and mystery is established:

> But what
> We cannot even find questions for
> Is how near we were: brushed by the same snow
> Lifted by her wake as she passed. We could

> Have spoken, we swear, with anyone on her deck,
> And had not to raise our voices, if we
> Had known anything to say. And now
> In no time at all, she has put
> All of disaster between us: a gulf
> Beyond reckoning. It begins where we are. (F, 210)

In the poem's opening lines nearness takes on a spiritual as well as a
literal and physical dimension. This "gulf / Beyond reckoning" is
lodged within ourselves. The final line implies that the gulf emanates
out from us, precluding all other intimacy. The recognition of closeness
to the mystery has precipitated the widening of the gulf. The void
between the speaker and any reader "begins where we are," where the
speaker is. What Merwin is discovering is an irrational distancing
which may attend the coming of profound knowledge, a distancing
like that of "the flat light rising." His incommunicable knowledge will
widen the gulf between himself and others until its scope is "Beyond
reckoning." This cleaving knowledge makes him adamantine regarding the other human beings who figure in his poems of shipwreck. He
sheds no tears for those 157 voyagers who lost their lives when the
Portland sank. As if it had all occurred in legend or myth, he can only
feel stark wonder, leaving the reader to experience a parallel isolation
from the poet: each reader senses he is on his own "*Portland* Going
Out."

In these sea poems contact with the mystery and silence of life
destroys all human value. Merwin emphasizes this in the cryptic poem
"Cape Dread": "But what we found / You will find for yourselves,
somewhere, for / Yourselves. We have not gone there again, / Nor
ventured ever so far again." (F, 213) Navigating deep into the psyche,
Merwin finds a place full of horror. He names it Cape Dread and will
say no more about it except to speculate on various names others might
choose for it. His response to finding it is to set limits on further exploration: "We have not gone there again, / Nor ventured ever so far
again." That is, at least until the next book, *The Moving Target*.

"The Frozen Sea," the last sea poem of *The Drunk in the Furnace*
to be considered here, intensifies and epitomizes that dread in the face
of the unknown. Wind here becomes the active principle of the mystery, confronting, even probing, the human explorer:

> We walked on it, in the very flesh
> No different only colder, as was

> The sea itself. It was simple as that.
> Only, the wind would not have it, would not
> Have it: the whiteness at last
> Bearing us up where we would go. Screamed
> With lungs we would never have guessed at,
> Shrieked round us, whipping up the cold crust,
> Lashing the rigid swell into dust. It would
> Find the waves for us, or freeze out
> The mortal flaw in us: it was not any light
> From heaven that hurt our eyes, but
> The whiteness that we could not bear. (F, 207)

This encounter with the hellish white of the frozen sea which attempted to "freeze out / The mortal flaw in us" is like Ahab's deadly struggle with the white whale; its chaos constitutes an apocalyptic testing.

In "White Goat, White Ram," Merwin associated whiteness with loss of reason and memory: "And we should say those are white who remember nothing" (F, 136). There whiteness characterized the void of lost intellect as here it characterizes the hell of total whiteness in the loss of sight. This is a blinding "whiteness that we could not bear," a whiteness which renders him, like Samson, "eyeless in Gaza." To succumb to the circular violence of the storm would mean succumbing to annihilation; it would imply "going under" mentally, "staying" in the madness of the churning psychic forces which engulf him:

> But danger
> Had given shape, stiffening shape, to our
> Pride, and that sustained us in silence
> As we went over that screaming silence.
> Yet how small we were around whom the howling
> World turned. (F, 206)

Only the clear and present danger forces the speaker to stiffen his pride and move on. Deliberate, possibly futile, motion eclipses his knowledge—or admission to consciousness—of the whiteness. Again, all human value and "Virtues" are annihilated.

At the end the speaker would seem to be freezing to death, losing in his struggle with the mystery, the silence. He is aware of his own insignificance in the face of this vastness: "Yet how small we were around whom the howling / World turned." He appears to be standing at the southernmost tip of the earth, the static central axis around which it

turns. At the moment of death—or at his brush with death—he reex-
periences "the terror / That cannot be charted, . . . only / A little of
it." "The Frozen Sea" ends: "We had come so far / To whiteness, and
it was cruel in our eyes, / To the pure south, and whichever way we
turned / Was north, the sides of the north, everywhere" (F, 207). He
defiantly persists in creating out of the void a meaning sustained by
silence, though he is locked in place visually and physically, if not mentally. Those who walk on the frozen sea, though retaining not much
more than their souls, are paradoxically guided only by "a soulless
needle." In a mystical sequence, the lines describe a giddy circular
motion paralleling the crazy motion of the compass needle in which
"whichever way we turned / Was north, the sides of the north, everywhere." He has arrived at the pure south just as he has arrived at the
simultaneous vacancy and illumination of total knowledge, which is
death.

Merwin has staked out the dangerous place where he wants to dwell
in his poetry: in years and poems to come he will be charting the terror,
dealing with the silence, which, he later declares, "is my shepherd"
(CL, 116). He will be trying to find the questions and answers for "how
near we were."

III   Pictures from the Merwin Family Album

Renegade and fugitive from polite drawing rooms, the author of
"Lemuel's Blessing" is himself the drunk in the furnace. In the latter
part of *The Drunk in the Furnace,* Merwin reviews his family, seeing
them with cold eyes which penetrate to the soul. He cannot abide his
family's rigid Protestant orthodoxy, their loveless grasping at salvation.
Merwin renders their consciousness in poems which recapture the telling moment between unconsciousness and waking; the scene is typically that of a grandfather dozing at a window. In each successive family portrait he depicts some ogre of his childhood. Malkoff speculates
that "some sort of liberating process took place" in this volume and
that it is not "simply a coincidence that the family poems immediately
precede the emergence of Merwin as a practitioner of open form."[11]
In breaking psychologically and emotionally with past lives—his own
and others'—Merwin frees himself of the traditional constraints of
poetic form as well.

His staid, strict father, the Presbyterian minister, the embodiment of
Christian social propriety, dominates his childhood. He was raised in

a quiet Victorian home where little emotion was expressed. A person brought up in such a home might well be subject to Robert Bly's criticism that "There are often no odors, or sounds, or senses, and the work is often barren of personality."[12] This comment on the early style also applies to much of the poetry published before *The Carrier of Ladders*. In Merwin's early work he maintained "a withdrawn, somewhat lofty perspective, almost God-like. That is, Merwin saw the world from above, looking down upon smaller things. He observed, described and made judgments about this world with which he seemed to have little direct contact."[13] Isn't this the stance of the proper Victorian, wary of the sensual or sensory dimension? In some respects Merwin adopted poetically the visage and voice of his aloof father. The book *The Drunk in the Furnace* frees him of the father and of the father's many allies in tyranny. In sloughing these off, he sloughs off the stricter formal requirements of the well-made poem as well. In the final section of this chapter, I shall show his progress toward the revelation of his future voice and poetic domain.

Respect for the power of the word—the words of adults as well as the Word of God or the Word made flesh—was instilled in Merwin early. His family had a straitlaced conception of what a good child or, for that matter, a good adult should be. It is ironic to observe that none of those featured in Merwin's family album seem inwardly to conform to the harsh demands they made on others to conform: they are hypocrites. All but the most senile secretly believe that the discipline and decorum they ask of others is unnecessary for themselves. Merwin presents a "decaying generation" of women who were hypocritically religious and men who were, if not pastors, drunkards. Is there subtle humor or malice in his dedicating *this* of all books to his parents?

As a child Merwin read adventure stories of the sea and medieval epics. Since this child was supposed to be seen and not heard, he voyaged in his imagination and spoke in poems. His first poems were hymns he wrote for his father.

The portrait of his grandmother presented in "Grandmother Watching at her Window" (F, 248) and "Grandmother Dying" (F, 249–51) is one of a senile woman glibly unaware of the inconsistencies in her character. Like the other poems treating his forebears, this is his assessment of and farewell to an important relative. Although grandmother has kept her love from her husband by shutting "my soul tight / Behind my mouth, so he could not steal it," still she taught her children "that stealing / Is the worst sin; [she] knew if I loved them / They

would be taken away." Her entire life has been a series of good-byes
to departing loved ones. Her consciousness of loss and dissolution, the
pain of division, is not so strong as that of the poet who tells her poignantly illogical tale.

Then there is "Grandfather in the Old Men's Home," which begins
sarcastically: "Gentle at last, and as clean as ever, / He did not even
need drink any more, / And his good sons unbent and brought him /
Tobacco to chew, both times when they came" (F, 247). Afterimages
of his relationship with his wife frequent his dreams:

> And he smiled all the time to remember
> Grandmother, his wife, wearing the true faith
> Like an iron nightgown, yet brought to birth
> Seven times and raising the family
> Through her needle's eye while he got away
> Down the green river, finding directions
> For boats. And himself coming home sometimes
> Well-heeled but blind drunk, to hide all the bread
> And shoot holes in the bucket while he made
> His daughers pump. (F, 248)

The needle's eye recalls the Biblical statement that it is as difficult for
a rich man to get into heaven as a camel to go through a needle's eye
and is an image for the grandmotherly discipline—"I brought the children up clean / With my needle" (F, 248). The children she bears she
pushes through the needle's eye into salvation. When he is not working
as a river pilot or getting drunk, grandfather comes home to make
sadistic demands on his daughters and "hide all the bread." The last
detail of the sequence, his shooting "holes in the bucket while he made
/ His daughters pump," is too bizarre to be anything but authentic.

Merwin conjures up his deathbed scene, grandmother attending:
"Huge in her age, with her thumbed-down mouth / Hating the river,
filling with her stare / His gliding dream, while he turned to water."
Water here represents the comparative fluidity and flexibility of his
character in the face of her frigidity: the river has always been his
escape from her, his freedom. And what else but water corrodes "an
iron nightgown"? Though she can fill "with her stare / His gliding
dream," he can at last merge with his dream and exist solely in it. As
he dies "the children they both had begotten / With old faces now,
but themselves shrunken / To child-size again, stood ranged at her
side, / Bearing their little Bibles till he died" (F, 247).

Fundamentalist religion, scrupulous neatness, a withholding of love, a narrow-minded discipline become Merwin's chief targets for ridicule in this portrait gallery. The best of the lot is "Uncle Hess" (F, 246) who named his "tall daughter for the goddess / Minerva, whom all agreed she resembled / Till her car smashed with her and Olympus crumbled." Certainly Olympus is not all that is crumbling in these ruthless poems. Christianity is exposed as a religion of fear, with God as a vengeful, ever-watchful killer in the skies. In "Small Woman on Swallow Street," a poem applauded by Robert Bly in *The Sixties*, we meet the fear-crazed Christian consciousness:

> A big coat
> Can help save you. But eyes push you down; never
> Meet eyes.
>
> . . . .
>
> Do not look up there:
> The wind is blowing the building tops, and a hand
> Is sneaking the whole sky another way, but
> It will not escape. Do not look up. God is
> On High. He can see you. You will die. (F, 241)

This woman has the same mixture of insanity and sharpness grandmother had. Once again, the emphasis is on shutting out the adversary by means of full-length clothes—here coats and furs. The needle-sharp eyes must be kept lowered for fear of seeing a hand "sneaking the whole sky another way." She is convinced that if she looks up, God will pounce on her and devour her. Her vision is hooded, nearly blinded, so narrow is its range. Significantly, blindness is the major symbol for spiritual myopia here: it operates effectively in "Blind Girl" which opens: "Silent, with her eyes / Climbing above her like a pair of hands drowning" (F, 237), and in "One-Eye," which takes for epigraph the line, "In the country of the blind the one-eyed man is king" (F, 239).

These narrowly orthodox Christians and advocates of free enterprise have no eyes nor names to see with. So broadly are they blind and lost, they can only hold by clutching and love by torturing those they love. Certainly Merwin's family is not unique as middle-class American families go. Grandmother dies, "And when she heaved up / Her last breath, to shake it like a fist, / . . . her chair went on / Rocking all by itself with nothing alive / Inside it to explain it, nothing, nothing" (F,

250–51). The mechanical void of her life is emphasized in the repetition of "nothing" at the end and in the soulless persistence of her chair's going on rocking without her.

In "The Native," a scathing summary of the life of an anonymous native of Merwin's Pennsylvania/New Jersey homeland, the poet assesses the whole tribe:

> ... the best
> Went west long ago, got out from under,
> Waved bye-bye to the steep scratched fields and scabby
> Pastures: their chapped plaster of newspapers
> Still chafes from the walls, and snags of string tattling
> Of their rugs trail yet from the stair-nails. The rest
> Never the loftiest, left to themselves,
>   Descended, descended. (F, 252)

Here again the terminal repetition echoes a judgment on the whole lot. Those who "got out from under" God and left behind their shares in the farmland have not had to suffer daily this specter of loss and degradation. The "small" women and men alone remain, and they "descended," always fearing God's descent upon them. It is understandable that Merwin would present a literary tribute to this dying generation, himself waving "bye-bye to the steep scratched fields and scabby / Pastures" and souls. He has gone West himself, in the various senses of that term. Not only does he choose to live in Hawaii, but he has also been dead to this life—to this strain and stain of his family—for twenty years.

IV   *"The Drunk in the Furnace"*

Having distinguished himself from the descendants, Merwin chooses for his poetic residence "the real dark" of the unknown, the mystery of life. He sums up the enigma of the known in this comment: "Daily the indispensable is taught to elude us, while we are furnished according to our wishes with armories of what we do not need" (H, 94). What he needs exists in the blind depths, the uncharted reaches to which he retreats from myth (Olympus and Minerva), the Protestant God, and other conventions imposed on him by civilized society. In the title poem of the book Merwin envisions how he might better explore the perimeters of the mysterious:

> For a good decade
> The furnace stood in the naked gully, fireless
> And vacant as any hat. Then when it was
> No more to them than a hulking black fossil
> To erode unnoticed with the rest of the junk-hill
> By the poisonous creek, and rapidly to be added
>   To their ignorance,
>   They were afterwards astonished
> To confirm, one morning, a twist of smoke like a pale
> Resurrection. (F, 261)

Merwin's conventional early style is "a hulking black fossil," "vacant as any hat." He does not personally inhabit any of the earlier poems. In fact, they are so objective, so mythic as to be anonymous. Although in 1960, he feels he has earned the reputation of a poet of stature, he knows if he persists in the exquisitely impersonal early style, he will rapidly be consigned to oblivion. He, like his ancestors, will be a relic of the past, rapidly be "added" to the sum of the world's "ignorance." His personal poetic voice is only here emerging in the guise of a "twist of smoke like a pale / Resurrection." This new life is "confirmed" by onlookers, the natives' "witless offspring" and critics. They begin to

> . . . remark then other tokens that someone
> Cosily bolted behind the eye-holed iron
> Door of the drafty burner, had there established
> His bad castle.   .
>   Where he gets his spirits
> It's a mystery. But the stuff keeps him musical!
> Hammer-and-anvilling with poker and bottle
> To his jugged bellowings, till the last groaning clang
> As he collapses onto the rioting
> Springs of a litter of car-seats ranged on the grates,
>   To sleep like an iron pig. (F, 261)

Richard Howard considers "The Drunk in the Furnace" "a fulfill-ment of the epigraph to *The Dancing Bears*, to wit, Flaubert's bitter observation that our speech is as the hammering on a cracked kettle to make bears dance, when we would seduce the stars." He sees it as a recording of "Merwin's advance—or is it a retreat?—to his own chaos from a borrowed or inherited order."[14] The order Merwin here estab-lishes for himself within the furnace is a domain where he makes

"religious, almost sacred noises with his bottle" and poker.[15] He then
passes into an alcoholic stupor and silence. The drunk sleeps in "His
bad castle" "like an iron pig." "Where he gets his spirits / It's a mystery." But the poem, like the drunk and Merwin's voice, is redeemed
by vitality and consistency.[16] "The Drunk in the Furnace" concludes:

> In their tar-paper church
> On a text about stoke-holes that are sated never
> Their reverend lingers. They nod and hate trespassers.
> When the furnace wakes, though, all afternoon
> Their witless offspring flock like piped rats to its siren
> Crescendo, and agape on the crumbling ridge
> Stand in a row and learn. (F, 261)

An immovable barrier is set up between poet and hearer. Henceforth
the poet will preach in "his juggled bellowing" on a "text about stoke-
holes"; the readers will "Stand in a row and learn." "The outside world
is in awe of the drunk and learns as much from his silence as from his
noise."[17] The welling, provident flow of his "music" is the central focus,
the only possible focus, of interest; it is the creative justification of the
drunk/poet's existence. "It is at this point that Merwin decided that he
no longer wishes merely to locate and observe the abyss; he wants to
explore it; he wants to become the drunk in the furnace. The furnace,
of course, is himself, his body and his inner life. To do this he knows
that his way of speaking must change. His poems must not merely
notice silence, they must to the extent possible, become silence. At least
they must be made of both the drunk's sacred thumping and stupor."
  Like the drunk in the furnace, Merwin sits in the darkness composing a poetry of absence, silence, and the clanging words that emerge
from his own chaos. It is a poetry comprised in part of "images of what
I never had." "It has taken me this long to learn what I cannot say /
where it begins like the names of the hungry" (CL, 28). His rolling
crescendos will display the mind in the process of finding meaning
within the furnace, finding words and spaces that will suffice to
account for his experience of it. He has been resurrected from the family "junk-hill," saved from "ignorance," so off and on he will continue
playing in the furnace even as the established orders of society, morality, poetry, and religion are crumbling like sinking ships. The assonance of "bad castle" signals the drunk's felicitous discovery of a cosy
home and hearth. He may remain here, educating the offspring in the

inward way of truth, teaching the innocent their "bad" catechism. Having found this new residence, he proclaims it as the home he will from time to time return to. In his next book, *The Moving Target*, published three years later, some poems come from within the furnace while some merely point out the scope of mystery and silence, "the terror which cannot be charted." If in the new book his aim is unsteady, after all a moving target is harder to hit.

CHAPTER 4

"Is That What You Are"

In a ruined time
one searches
for a searing language
that's torn
fragmented.
Jean Follain

IN *The Moving Target* (1963), Merwin surrenders the notion of completeness in life and in art. He surrenders the idea that his life can
or must be completed or fulfilled according to traditional American
measures of success and fulfillment. Although Yeats admonished that
a poet must "choose perfection of the life or of the art," still Merwin
swings wide of any perfectionism in the Surrealist outburst of this new
book. Here instead we find the detritus of a psychic crisis which signals
a stylistic and inward revolution. In it he severs ties with conventionality in life and in art. No longer an apprentice in the craft of verse,
he renounces Pound, Auden, Eliot, Graves, even Lowell, the old
models. Tired of a style that by now is coming to seem merely imitative and hackneyed, Merwin moves into open forms. This move has
marked the career of every major American poet who began publishing in the 1950s—James Wright, Denise Levertov, Adrienne Rich, A.
R. Ammons, James Dickey, W. D. Snodgrass, and even Anne Sexton,
whose first book actually didn't appear until 1960.

All these poets left behind Modernism and its aesthetic tenets. All
responded to a disordered time and to the war in Viet Nam by writing
increasingly disordered poetry. All relinquished the notion that one's
life or one's poem should be cast in a carefully crafted, self-consistent
form. Formally, W. S. Merwin set out for "the desert of the unknown"
like "Noah's Raven," thereby opening the field for a revolution in his
own style and sensibility. Because it is his own original voice he elects
to speak in, he insists in "singing" alone. The opposite of the prodigal
son of whom he wrote so movingly in *Green with Beasts*, like the wolf

76

Lemuel, who embodies exile, he becomes a hoarder of himself and his own vital resources. The result is an independent, original poetry which bears a closer resemblance to the poetry of René Char, Pierre Reverdy, Francis Ponge, or Gay Michaux than to that of any prior American with the possible exception of Lawrence Ferlinghetti.

Besides introducing Merwin's outrageous, courageous new style, part Surrealist manifesto, part psalm, part curse, *The Moving Target* also inducted Merwin into a true intimacy with death and nothingness. In *The Drunk in the Furnace* death simply inspired the horror of profound recognition. But to Merwin's heightened cultural consciousness, death becomes the foundation of any poem treating contemporary American culture. It is the necessary subject of any poem evoking the experience of living in the world's most materialistic nation today since the worship of materialism is a worship of death. But despite his intimacy with death, death remains as frightening for Merwin as Jean-Paul Sartre's *le néant*. It is never the comfortable merging with the vegetable kingdom in organic dissolution: "When Roethke or Bly write about death, it becomes desirable, . . . lovable, not so much because it leads to new life—as it may in some traditional mystic poets,—but because it creates a corporeal union with the flow of time and matter into eternity. . . . What death is for Merwin is suggested by the very different image . . . 'the black mouth / of the first nothing.' Here is the blank heart of Merwin's fascination: death considered not as a way to union but as the entrance to nothing, which for him is more obsessively present than any of the things which it is not."[1]

To account for death, the "entrance to nothing," *The Moving Target* devises a negative aesthetic. He forges an aesthetic construct not of what is, but of what is not, "the terror which cannot be charted." Misunderstanding this has led many critics, Robert Bly and Robert Peters among them, to misconstrue his poetic motives. But Merwin is plain in stating his intentions: he says, *"I know nothing / learn of me"* (CL, 51), and in the fine poem "For Now" he writes, "Tell me what you see vanishing and I / Will tell you who you are" (MT, 93). In his "mind of winter," abstractions participate in concrete images to build an antiworld, a world comprised of concretions which themselves are voids. Only negations and absences made physical and substantive can register the impact of the void of death on modern consciousness. Death is the First National obscenity: the American people hasten away from acknowledging it. Through creative incorporation of absences and negation into the poem, what is *can* be obliquely, if neg-

atively, defined through a delineation of what is not. What is not illu-
minates as it sunders what is by connecting it to the calcinating force
of the void. The resultant destruction of what had seemed a solidly
constructed world is all the more threatening because it occurs in
poetry noted for its relaxed, conversational style. In an elegy for his
elder sister, Jane Kirstein, a voice addresses her:

> By now you will have met
> no one
> my elder sister
> you will have sat
> by her breath in the dark
> she will have told you I don't know what (CL, 103)

In *The Moving Target* and its sequel *The Lice* (1967), Merwin finds
a way of moving in and through the void toward possible self-transcendence; in accepting the void of death as a friend, his poetic consciousness is freed to shoot into its vacancy and hit the poem. He
explores the interstices between the objects of materialistic desire,
sounding the depths of "silence," "emptiness," "no one," "nobody."
And he is confident, even feisty in his attacks on American piggishness.
He has no teacher but his own originality: "Now all my teachers are
dead except silence" (L, 50). Reckless courage and taunt songs characterize the psalmic new style: "My friends without shields walk on the
target" (MT, 80).

These negations are the product of his growing awareness of spiritual and cultural dispossession. Merwin's belief that America as a
nation has taken a wrong turning during the latter half of this century
introduces a tension and tautness into the poetry. His insights into the
"shimmering vista of emptiness" at the heart of American culture
imprint the lines with searing irony. In *The Lice* this alienation
increases, expressing itself in veiled political blasphemies against poli-
ticians who offer the wrong kind of insurance.

In writing these books, he draws on the pain caused by the poetic
and personal conformity he has submitted to in the past. Consequently,
along with death, time and memory become absolutes to him, corrosive
forces of the first magnitude; each is personified and given local habitation. He settles down to live with them in an uncanny *ménage à
trois*.

Before further investigating the role of nothingness in the new style, we will consider briefly the parallels between Merwin's and Yeats's changes of style.

I   *Walking Naked: Parallels with Yeats*

Merwin signals his stylistic independence in a poem from *The Moving Target* entitled "Standards" which begins: "Nothing will do but / I must get a new flag, / I've buried enough under this one" (MT, 52). The metaphor links style with a battle standard bearing his insignia or coat of arms. The observation, "I've buried enough under this one" sounds sinister; he speaks like a war-weary general feeling a desire for change. The fact that much has been "buried" under the old style is revealing: is he implying that the new style will be even more revealing? The bareness of these lines themselves states that the new style will be free of the elegant ornamentation that marked the old style. And it states that the new style will be more candid and direct, less meditative and long-winded.

A similar stylistic shift occurs in Yeats's poetry. Like Yeats, Merwin's early poems were "a masque about a vision." Perusing the early poetry of each, the reader is confronted with poems about visionary experiences, poems which do not treat of the experiences directly, but which delight in the harmonies of interweaving thought and emotion. Their emphasis is on fitly chosen, if archaic words, on languid rhythms and slack rhymes. The goal of the poetry is to render a vague sense of the transcience of life and beauty. Richard Howard comments that reading Merwin of this period is like attending to "orbific music which might charm into an imaginative unity all the disparates of experience."[2]

Just as the elaborately constructed poetry of the first books yielded to the more declarative, objective poetry displaying what Marianne Moore calls "a gallantry of observation" in *Green with Beasts*, so in *The Moving Target* Merwin's work undergoes a stunning stylistic change. He now writes constantly in the first person, and the language has taken a simpler, more generic turn. When he says in "Daybreak," "The future woke me with its silence / I join in the procession / An open doorway / Speaks for me / Again," he is saying that henceforth a simpler, more basic language will reflect his passage into exile. It will *be* exile. "From now on the open door of the furnace will speak for him. He lets us know that he is beginning to feel comfortable and at home within the interior. There will be no more vacillation, no more coming out for air."[3] The voice of the poem is the voice of the voluntary exile, Noah's raven, who boasts "the future / Splits the present with the echo of my voice" (MT, 10).

Perhaps the best *poetic* expression of Merwin's transformation appeared fifty years before the actual transformation in Yeats's "A Coat," written on his own change in style:

> I made my song a coat
> Covered with embroideries
> Out of old mythologies
> From heel to throat;
> But the fools caught it,
> Wore it in the world's eyes
> As though they'd wrought it.
> Song, let them take it,
> For there's more enterprise
> In walking naked.[4]

Both poets choose to shed the coat of the "old mythologies," windy rhetoric, which "fools caught," held up to be the standard of the poet himself, and imitated. The coat of each poet's style had been too much aped by fools who "Wore it in the world's eyes / As though they'd made it."

No one can mimic your coat if you walk naked. Tearing off the ornate "embroideries," each finds "there's more enterprise / In walking naked." Merwin leaves behind his dependence on earlier models of the 1950s and launches out into the open sea of a new style, sporting a new standard. Fifty years before, Yeats, feeling the winds of war within Ireland and in Europe, announced a new, harder, colder style, honed clean for battle. Each new style faces the challenges of the present rather than languishing in the "old mythologies." Each poet writes in a simpler, less contrived diction, using the real language of men speaking to men. In opening his ears to the language of the streets, each moves from art "wrought" in a closed field to creation in an open field.

The word "enterprise" in the last line of "A Coat" recalls the commercial lingo of businessmen, for whom "free enterprise" may evoke visions of Nirvana. In this context, however, the word draws on its first English meanings as defined in the *Oxford English Dictionary:* "A bold, arduous, or momentous undertaking" or "disposition to engage in undertakings of difficulty, risk or danger; daring spirit." The word evokes the crusader who sallies forth from his castle keep to wrestle with dragons and infidels. Yeats consciously alludes to the Romantic tradition of the man of courage unafraid to meet his adversaries and detractors in open combat. Instead of wearing the armor of encrusted poetic ornament, the poet finds "enterprise in walking naked." Paradoxically, his very vulnerability renders him shockingly invulnerable.

Surprisingly similar to "A Coat" is "Choice of Prides" from *The Drunk in the Furnace,* a poem by Merwin which trumpets the same message to the opposition, but which develops an even more militaristic imagery and stance:

> To tell the truth, it would have its points
> (Since fall we must) to do it proud:
> To ride for your fall on a good mount
> Hung with honors and looped garlands,
> Moved by the crowd's flattering sounds,
> Or to advance with brash din, banners,
> Flights of arrows leaping like hounds.
>
> But from a choice of prides I would pick
> (Or so I hope) the bare cheek
> To amble out, innocent of arms
> And alone, under the cocked guns
> Or what missiles might be in season,
> And this in the pure brass of the act
> Attired, and in no other armor.
> Considering that, of every species
> (I should reason) mine is most naked,
> For all its draperies enacting
> As a pink beast its honest nature,
> I will take in this raw condition
> What pride I can, not have my boast
> In glad-rags, my bravery plated.
>
> And I should think myself twice lucky
> (Stuck with my choice) if I could be sure
> That I have been egged on by nothing
> But neat pride, and not (as is common,)
> Brought to it by the veiled promptings
> Of vanity, or by poverty
> Or the fecklessness of despair. (F, 233–34)

Yeats has written a better poem on the subject: the simplicity of "A Coat"'s statement makes for a corresponding universality. All that is subtly implied in the Yeats poem is explicit in the strutting "Choice of Prides." The brevity of "A Coat" better equips it to express the themes of courage and "Honest nature." In Merwin's poem too many details cloak the basic meaning: "the crowd's flattering sounds," "brash din, banners," "looped garlands" are all descriptive devices which advance the narrative, and serve to celebrate the "pure brass" of his act, but which do not advance the piece intellectually or poetically.

The contrast between the old armored self and the prouder naked authentic self and poetic voice provides the basic conflict in each poem. "Neat pride," which is conveyed in the tone of the Yeats poem, is blatantly and stridently acclaimed in the Merwin poem. Pride seems to be the motive of the latter, whereas simply showing up the "fools" is the motive of the former. Here in question is the pride that empowered David to face Goliath. In a perhaps overly defensive flourish, Merwin imagines that even the most modern weaponry ("what missiles might be in season") may be arrayed against his nakedness. The warrior stands "enacting / As a pink beast its honest nature, / . . . in this raw condition." Ultimately, he states, he would hope not to have his "bravery plated" with "the veiled promptings / Of vanity, or by poverty / Or the fecklessness of despair." The talk here is more of armor than of an embroidered coat. The speaker feels a strong desire to ward off the thrusts of his opponents; this is not the sage poet of the Irish poem but a knight who secretly lusts for righteous combat, a crusader against the infidels. It seems that the gentleman doth protest too much.

Obviously Merwin seeks to arouse the reader's sympathy with his reference to his body as "a pink beast." Other appeals to the reader are made in the parenthetical phrases that occur at the beginning of each stanza's second line. These are distracting, even intrusive in that they assume a greater intimacy than the reader can honestly feel, given the brash mood of the poem. Even the last stanza appears to be a kind of parenthetical utterance, the poet speaking to himself; like the speaker in "Lemuel's Blessing," he pleads to his own private tutelary deity to preserve him from corruption. Is he *so* afraid that he will succumb?

Unlike its Irish forebear, the American poem is not tightly rhymed, though it, like the Irish poem, works on assonance and consonance. While the Yeats poem contains true rhymes, many of Merwin's are slack rhymes; but Merwin's "Considering that" echoes the same phrase in Yeats's "Prayer for my Daughter."

The poem's style and voice, each says, should reflect honest nature. In so asserting, each takes fearlessness as his standard. Each banishes the thought of imitating any prior writer. Ironically, Merwin's poem is close enough to Yeats's to warrant our assumption that even in declaring his independence from the past, he is clearly dependent on it for ideas and precedents. The choice of prides has been made before him.

On the other hand, in his poems on the change of style in *The Moving Target* Merwin's style and theme prove to be far less imitative. Visually, the poems of the new book present an absorbing, original spectacle: gone is the regular rectangular stanza and block of narrative, gone is the regular righthand margin, gone the syntactical links, gone the attempts at slack rhyme which figured in *The Drunk in the Furnace*. The poems appear to have exploded onto the page, the remnants of a psychic crisis. Howard believes these poems register the "ecstacy of identity on the brink of ash."[5] Here the poet has not troubled to clear up the debris, as Yeats or even the younger Merwin would have done. Consistent with the military imagery and mood of the preceding poem, though, is the ensign image of "Standards":

> Nothing will do but
> I must get a new flag,
> I've buried enough under this one,
>
> And then there are my
> Followers, mad for a bit of color,
> Damn them, . . .
> Maybe I thought
> I could go on and on flying the same flag,
> Like a fire,
> But it's faded white and I'm
> Not the fire, I'll have to find
> Something bright and simple to signify
> Me, what an order.
>
> What an order but I'll have to do something.
> Up until now the pulse
> Of the stone was my flag
> And the stone's in pieces. (MT, 52)

Howard observes, regarding "Standards," "Merwin himself is not beyond, or above, a certain rueful coquetry in the matter of his new poetics."[6] While the first stanza asserts the need for personal change, inner exigencies ("I've buried enough under this one") as well as the exigencies of form dictating a change, the fourth stanza speaks in a far more open, candid voice than any heard before. Here is the language we all hear and speak every day.

He will accept a new standard not because pride impels it but because his followers are "mad for a bit of color, / Damn them." The choice is almost passive in the final stanzas which take on a more ruminative, private tone, the tone which is unique to *The Moving Target*. His treatment of the subject is rueful, resigned: "And the end I suppose is not yet, / The way the trees come beating / Their horses, and the wheat is camped / Under the dead crow." He is not totally passive, however: "And I'm not ready / To just sit down and let the horizon / Ride over me." But the old fire and protest have gone out of him: "the pulse / Of a stone" was his old flag, and that stone pulse is now silent for "the stone's in pieces." (I think this line may echo the lines "Enchanted to a stone" and "The stone's in the midst of all," from "Easter 1916" by Yeats.) Merwin's stone represents the paralyzing force of artifice. In leaving behind artifice, he greets a new informality in form: verbal contractions, the first person pronoun, long winding rhythmical lines, and a more intense handling of imagery give the poetry a new lightness and intimacy.

II   *The New Style: The Bombing of Versailles*

> When Israel went into exile, so did its language.
>   Saying from the Zohar

With the exception of Edward Dorn,[7] critics have hailed the advent of Merwin's new style as a triumph of authenticity. James Dickey asserted that the poems bear "the handprint of necessity."[8] Writing five years later, Richard Howard in *Alone with America* notes that the images are "arranged so that the lines never enclose but instead expose them."[9] Images hit the reader at the end of the lines or hang suspended between lines, ready to strike like cobras. Lines themselves, Howard notes, are "almost ideograms," he observes a "fiercer alienation," a "more convulsive diction."[10]

Malkoff, writing a few years later, discovers a richer depth of nuance in *The Moving Target* and signals the chief advance as "The creation of a language that operates as a universe in itself, and not merely as a medium by which thought is expressed."[11] Yet as René Char says in a poem Merwin translated just before this period, "Nothing had heralded so strong an existence."[12]

What exactly is Merwin's new form? What new skins hold the wine? He has abandoned narrative to adopt a Surrealist use of "exploding" images, images which detonate sequentially as one reads through the poem. Instead of using narrative to weld the poem together into a formal whole, he now depends on imagery to sustain the development of thought and emotion. There is no effort to connect the imagery logically: images undergo protean transformations. The second to the last stanza of "Air" provides a typically bizarre series which is well integrated thematically, tonally, and rhythmically:

> I forget tomorrow, the blind man.
> I forget the life among the buried windows.
> The eyes of the curtain.
> The wall
> Growing through the immortelles.
> I forget silence
> The owner of the smile. (MT, 50)

The rhetorical and philosophical speculations of the first four books ran underground only to well up again in jets of emotionally charged thought and imagery. His aversion to rigid conventionality and dull-witted orthodoxy finds outlet in explosions of violent imagery and powerful renunciation. If in the first two books he was obsessed by the power of the imagination to create, here he is obsessed by the power of the word or image to destroy. In throwing aside narrative, he gives up trying to construct a story to explain events, as he did in *The Drunk in the Furnace*. He reverts to native feeling and to a dwelling on—and in—failures, vacancies, reversal, and accidence. This bitter strain will deepen and broaden in his two books of prose, *The Miner's Pale Children* (1970) and *Houses and Travellers* (1977). In these works the bitterness bursts the bonds of the poem altogether and runs into prose; it is significant that Merwin's first prose is published in *The Moving Target*.

The focus of the poem has shifted from thought to feeling, from the general to the particular or the singular, from narrative to vital, passionately charged imagery, from stilted diction to dynamic everyday language. All normal orders of speech, idiom, and thought are in upheaval in *The Moving Target* and *The Lice*. In fact, Merwin

delights in reversing clichés so as to shock the reader out of the stupor
of following routines: "I come home as web to its spider" (MT, 39).
Mary Helen Slowik argues, "Like the Surrealists, Merwin is interested
in jarring the spatial and temporal contexts of images so that the physical, surface world, usually understood according to pre-existing orders,
suddenly points to hidden meanings."[13] Experiencing a logical or idi-
omatic order reversed shocks the reader into a new perception of the
cool deceptiveness of language and life.

Jarold Ramsey comments on the private nature of the poetry: "We
find here the mind's first unpurposive gathering of images and words
before it is forced to move towards concepts, conclusions, public utterance."[14] Shards and fragments remain for the lover of puzzles to piece
together. Quick cinematic shifts of image, mood, and idea prevail. The
reader, precipitated into thought, is forced to "build a world of snow,"
a world of nothingness. The reader forges his own coherence. The
value of the poem resides, as William Carlos Williams declared, in "the
minute organization of the words and their relationships," in the minute intimations of thought and emotions, *not* in any public utterance
or "message" conveyed. In "The Gods" Merwin offers a kind of expla-
nation for his poetic "occupation":

> If I have complained I hope I have done with it
>
> I take no pride in circumstances but there are
> Occupations
> My blind neighbor has required of me
> A description of darkness
> And I begin I begin but . . .
>
> The gods are what has failed to become of us
> Now it is over we do not speak
>
> Now the moment has gone it is dark
> What is man that he should be infinite
> The music of a deaf planet
> The one note
> Continues clearly this is
>
> The other world
> These strewn rocks belong to the wind
> If we could use them (L, 30–31)

His goal is to describe the darkness, to account for what exists in these dark interiors, what *is* and what *is not*, down in the darkness of the self's core where he makes his music. Genuine contemplation of darkness leads to a contemplation and understanding of light; hearing silence makes him attentive to the "music of a deaf planet." In that contemplation resides the secret of creativity and renewal.

In *The Moving Target* and *The Lice* the poet ceases to use description as a means of imparting some knowledge external to the poem itself. Nor do events or scenes of natural disasters serve any longer as a pretext for making a philosophical commentary on life or on human beings in general, as they did in "Burning the Cat," "Uncle Hess," "The Burning Mountain," etc. Objects, events, or scenes do not emerge physically from the poem; they remain implicit in it, fixed in the imagery. They are employed for their connotative rather than for their denotative meanings. Instead of being objects, they are actually subjects, parts of a whole internal order of experience. Thus in "The Finding of Reasons" the "waves" operate as subjects without referents: "Every memory is abandoned / As waves leave their shapes / The houses stand in tears as the sun rises" (L, 74). The metaphor equates loss of memory with loss of shape. The water is appropriately transformed into tears in the third line. The connection established is a connection between the images and ideas inherent in the poem rather than a truth that can be detached from it.

The setting of all Merwin poems from *The Moving Target* to *Writings to an Unfinished Accompaniment* is rendered in "The Room": "I think all this is somewhere in myself / The cold room unlit before dawn / Containing a stillness such as attends death" (L, 48). For a decade most of Merwin's poetry will inhabit this room which is "somewhere in myself": "And from a corner the sounds of a small bird trying / From time to time to fly a few beats in the dark / You would say it was dying it is immortal." Merwin has shed the mask of artificial form which hid his true face and voice. Now the reader meets not only the self behind the mask but the soul—and the stillness—dwelling within.

III   *Negations: Zeros on the Account*

W. S. Merwin's radical embrace of negations, his writing on the void, becomes prominent in *The Moving Target* and becomes obsessional in *The Lice*. Slowik explains, "Like the earliest spokesman of the Surrealist movement, Apollinaire, even like its most influential forebears, Baudelaire and Rimbaud, Merwin embraces negation as an essential quality of an absolute which can be known only through the contradictions and absences it introduces into our limited world."[15] As in the poetry of Apollinaire, Baudelaire, and Rimbaud, the absolute is not beyond negation but includes it and can only be identified through it. Merwin approaches that absolute through introducing contradictions, voids, and absences into the poem.

Slowik elucidates his adoption of Surrealism as the only viable means of imaging his inner crisis and comprehension of reality: "And in the later books, *The Moving Target, The Lice, The Carrier of Ladders,* and *Writings to an Unfinished Accompaniment,* both the gothic extravagance and the shadows emerge into a Surrealism which brings the speaker into intimate contact with the deaths he sees around him and yet makes of this contact a way of moving into and through the void toward possible self-transcendence. . . ."[16] Merwin viscerally experiences the deaths manifesting themselves in modern technological culture, as Apollinaire did. Merwin's poetry reflects his apprehension of them in a radical incorporation of negation into the poem. A brief look at his embodiment of nothingness in his first poems will show the roots of this practice and the growth of his negative aesthetic.

As early as *A Mask for Janus,* he had imaged a "vain country" where all natural orders are reversed. Substantial concrete realities appear "vain" of substance "in savorless repose." They evaporate even as the poem progresses:

> There is no breath of days . . .
> in that place, through the trees;
> no winds nor satellites,
> seasons nor bodies rise;
> are no descent of rivers,
> wavering of fishes,
> indecision of tides,
> langor before pause,
> nor any dance to please,
> nor prayers, pleasure of knees,
> coupling, smile of increase,
> swaying of fruit and seas, . . .
> but that vain country lies
> in savorless repose. (F, 47–48)

Even time and the natural cycles are negated through this utter absence of corporeality: "no breath of days / . . . no . . . seasons . . .

rise." The poem's world is a spiritual world where things are nonexistent and "disstated."[17] And, though admittedly Merwin partially dissociates himself from this world in the poem, in view of the attitude toward human beings and human relationships expressed here and in "Dictum: For a Masque of Deluge," it is easy to see how Richard Howard could write of the latter poem and, we may think, of this poem too: "Sexuality . . . the actual life of the body, . . . is not so much disallowed as disbelieved; the very rhythms of the stanza have a kind of wandering fainéance about them."[18] In the envoi of "Sestina" in *The Dancing Bears*, Merwin writes of his own physical existence and reality: "A breathed name I was with no resting-place, / A bough of sleep that had no share of morning, / Till I had made a body and a season from a song" (43). "Body and season," one's personal identity, fulfillment, and "time" are made from a song: firm physical reality, "body," inheres in the song itself. Characteristic of Merwin's first two books is a disbelief in the physical life of the body or of objects and a belief in the solidity of aesthetic realities.

Similarly, in *The Moving Target* objects do not exist as independent external entities. Since the poetry is written in the Surrealist language of transformation, all concrete objects are given new meanings and significations by the poet's powerful transfiguring imagination. In "Recognition," a poem published in *The Moving Target* in 1963, the variety of objects mentioned operates to construct and create within the poem a psychic state, "un paysage d'âme" or soul's landscape; but none of the objects has a secure or solid existence in the external world:

> The bird of ash has appeared at windows
> And the roads will turn away, mourning.
> What distances we survived, the fire
> With its one wing
> And I with my blackened heart
>
> I came home as a web to its spider,
> To teach the flies of my household
> Their songs. I walked
> In on the mirrors scarred as match-boxes,
> The gaze of the frames and the ticking
> In the beams. The shadows
> Had grown a lot and they clung
> To the skirts of the lamps.
> Nothing
> Remembered who I was.

> The dead turn in their locks and
> I wake like a hand on a handle. Tomorrow
> Marches on the old walls, and there
> Is my coat full of darkness in its place
> On the door.
> Welcome home,
> Memory. (MT, 39)

Here imaginative abstractions assume the physical reality usually attributed to objects; they act. "Nothing" stands sinisterly in the doorway. Alone in its line, it becomes the subject of the next lines, actively remembering "who I was." Yet it cannot grasp "who I *am*." In Merwin's cosmology things "Appear / not as they are / but as what prevents them" (CL, 118).

The speaker and the fire have survived "distances," it "With its one wing / And I with my blackened heart." His burnt-out heart may be the result of the combustion of memories. Instead of returning home as the proverbial spider to its web, the speaker *is* the returning nest of associations and images, the web which does not exist independent of him. He comes home "as a web to its spider," home is the spider which centers him. The shadows which have "grown a lot" are naturally cobwebs. Images of watchfulness prevail: the mirrors and the "gaze of the frames and the ticking / In the beams" are all sources of vision and measures of time expired. Self-knowledge grows as the web returns to haunt and *be* him. The "Recognition" effected is a self-recognition.

Starkly modern personification—"Nothing / Remembered" him—combines with classical irony and paradox to achieve superb poetic effects. Instead of being greeted by the house's watchful denizens, *he* exclaims: "Welcome home, / Memory." Like charity, memory begins at home. But it is not images of the past that parade on the walls but images of the future: "Tomorrow / Marches on the old walls."

Just as in "Recognition," "Nothing" and "Tomorrow" and "Memory" figure as subjects acting and reacting in the poem, so Merwin invests "silence" and "emptiness" with physical presence and dynamic traits in other poems. He first uses this paradoxical literary device in *Green with Beasts*, speaking of "silence bursting beyond that clamor" (156). And in the next book the poem "The Frozen Sea" alludes to "that screaming silence" (207). Later, in *The Lice*, "A Scale in May" begins "Now all my teachers are dead except silence / I am trying to read what the five poplars are writing / On the void" (50), and he asserts, "I will take with me the emptiness of my hands / What you do not have you find everywhere" (55). Even more intriguing is his use of these abstractions to denote persons: "I thought it was an empty doorway / standing there by me / and it was you" (CL, 111).

To emphasize his will to transform the material world and his lack of faith in the only *apparently* solid concrete objects he sees around him, Merwin constructs a new physical universe of negations. His poetry focuses more steadily on the private inner world of the self. He builds a corresponding private world of vague, colorless negatives which move and act more positively and significantly than do the objects of the tangible, physical world. We observe a related tendency to define clear concepts or abstractions in negative terms: "Distance / is where we were / but empty of us and ahead of us" (CL, 15).

Names now become another target of Merwin's negative aesthetic. For him neither words nor names ever seem to fit what they signify. This is because memory does not work. In "For Now" from *The Moving Target* he writes: "Mistakes in the mail Goodbye to the same name / Goodbye what you learned for me I have to learn anyway / You that forgot your rivers they are gone / Myself I would not know" (90). Human beings have not yet found the language where names actually correspond to things. The poet can only try to invent this primal language. He is restricted by the limited, imprecise tools at hand. And sometimes sheer ignorance of conventional names and customs can be a source of strength and salvation. His negative aesthetic, characterized by the embodiment of negation in the poetry, is forged from his silence and ignorance—"With all my words my silence being one" (MT, 90)—in the hope that silence will save humanity now that positivism and capitalism have failed. This conviction is implicit in "The Saint of the Uplands":

> I took a single twig from the tree of my ignorance
> And divined the living streams under
> Their very houses. I showed them
> The same tree growing in their dooryards
> You have ignorance of your own, I said
> They have ignorance of their own. (MT, 17)

The poet/saint "divined the living streams under / Their very houses," showing them their "ignorance." This ignorance is intuition: it is the heart's intelligence in dealing with that part of reality that we feel, but do not name or rationally know. No emotion, no strong feeling can ever be named precisely; yet the poet does render emotion and feeling in poetry. He remains in touch with "the living streams under our very houses." The saving lesson that "Learning a Dead Language" teaches is "what sense of yourself / Is memorable, what passion may be heard / When there is nothing for you to say" (F, 177). Knowledge exists in the subliminal connections we make; it can be imparted like music, but Merwin disbelieves in our conventional systems of education. Conscious knowledge is of less importance to him than the precognitive illuminations which are the raw material of his poetry. The substance of poetry is that which cannot be named directly, discursively, or precisely, but which can be communicated prerationatively. Mallarmé was aware of the symbolic dimension of the page: black print is interpenetrated by the white of silence or absence of communication. Likewise, Merwin is aware that all true poetry and true communication are interlaced with the silence, the deep, nameless iceberg of which language is only the tip:

> I take in my arms
>
> My love whose names I cannot say
> Not knowing them and having a tongue
> Of dust . . .
>
> We say good-bye distance we are here
> We can say it quietly who else is there
> We can say it with silence our native tongue. (MT, 78–79)

Since we cannot speak in the primal language, our tools of communication are limited. Poets and composers set down what they hear and feel at the subliminal junction of names, notes, or words and human sensibility. And yet the very act of writing has the effect of ordering the raw materials of words, ideas, sounds, rhythms, and movements. Thus "The first composer / could hear only what he could write" (CL, 115). And, in a sense, anyone can hear and know only that which he can express in one form or another. Of the brief poem about the first composer, Evan Watkins says, "Its subject is the secret of the power of metaphor, the dramatic simplification and fusion that is 'first,' primary, what 'to compose' means at its root."[19] Only the astute poet/composer skillfully uses metaphor to make reality and poetic knowledge more hearable and knowable.

Merwin's grievance against things is that they distract his attention from hearing "what he could write"; they divert him from the inner voice of the self, the music in the furnace. By drawing the mind to the external man-made world, they disrupt and destroy the intuitive silence and "ignorance" from which true wisdom springs. And it is through silence that he finds himself. In a poem from the series "Words from a Totem Animal," he addresses silence:

> Stars even you
> have been used
> but not you
> silence
> blessing
> calling me when I am lost (CL, 19)

IV   The Lice

The music of a deaf planet

Evan Watkins comments on the bitter renunciation Merwin articulates in *The Lice:*

> The extent of Merwin's renunciation is most direct in *The Lice,* published in 1967 and one of the most important books of poetry to appear in the sixties. The year also marked the national emergence of The Doors and Jimi Hendrix, the March on the Pentagon, the publication of Ihab Hassan's study of Henry Miller and Beckett, and it was in this sibilant whir of immanent apocalypse that Merwin had realized already the falseness of escaping one order of finality merely to institute another. *The Lice* is filled with disgust at all things human and an accompanying awareness of the impossibility that our humanness can ever be dissolved into the vast, unspoken darkness of a waiting kingdom.[20]

Presumably, he refers to waiting vegetable and animal kingdoms of burial and decay. Watkins quotes the last line of "Avoiding News by the River": "If I were not human I would not be ashamed of anything" (L, 71).

The Lice registers the sensibility of a poet empty of the *Logos*-like love that animated the early books. Here his knowledge is not love-inspired or love-directed but a knowledge of hatred and bitterness. In this book Merwin is a poet pitted against the commercial greed and technological destructiveness of the American republic to which after forty years he has still not succeeded in acclimating himself. He sees lice on the body politic—in the most embarrassing parts. A riddle from

Heraclitus in the book's epigraph serves as his rallying cry and standard: "What we have caught and what we have killed we have left behind, but what has escaped us we bring with us." The living poet speaking to an unintelligent public identifies the lice we have brought with us into the present, those which may have eluded efforts at extermination. With the escalation of the Viet Nam War, he witnesses the lice of hatred and internecine war, lice the republic thought it had killed in its race for progress. He publishes "The Asians Dying," "Peasant," "Some Last Questions," "When the War is Over" (L, 63, 65, 6, 64).

In "Unfinished Book of Kings" he employs negations to express the conviction that prophets—and human values—are "without honor in their own country." The prophets of his poem die and go unattended; similarly, poets who prophesy ruin go unheard:

III Silence the last of the liberty ships had come up the river during the
    night and tied up to wait until the wharf rotted away

IV At that time the civil war between the dynasties of absence had been
    going on for many years

V But during that winter the lips of the last prophets had fallen from the
    last trees . . .

VII And in spite of the little votes burning at the altars in front of the
    empty wells

VIII And the jailers' eagle headed keys renewed in the name of freedom

IX It had been many years since the final prophet had felt the hand of the
    future how it had no weight and had realized that he the prophet was
    a ghost and had climbed the cracks in the light to take his place with
    the others . . .

XI The feet of the prophets fell but were not visible since their goal had
    ceased to exist. (L, 13)

The lamenting tone of "Alpha," the poem's opening section, is the tone of the entire book: Merwin, the last prophet, mourns the loss of a higher code of values. Having lost not just the means to attain it but even the goal itself, the poem's "last prophet" climbs "the cracks in the light to take his place with the others." The detail of "the jailers' eagle headed keys" sets the scene in the contemporary United States, and the "civil war between two dynasties of absence" alludes to the civil war then being waged in Viet Nam. The "little votes burning at the altars" reveal the callow piety of those who *believe* their votes mean something in a time when "the assurances proceeding from the mouths of presidents" are placebos as meaningless and futile as "the money pinned thick as tobacco fish over the eyes of the saints." Graft and corruption are the going price one pays for political achievement. Witnessing this, the prophets lose their lips, fingers, and feet. No one notices the fingers because they have no rings to dazzle the mercenary.

In "Beta" the reader finds a landscape of death. Here even the bones of the extinct horses are more perceptive of change and more sensitive to loss than the American public: "Before daybreak in the museums the skeletons of extinct horses held up the skeletons of extinct leaves to listen" (L, 14). Only this semblance of life lived in the darkness and concealment of the museums attests to the existence of the absolute. As manifested by the ghosts of what the human race has destroyed, death becomes a source of bitter lament, psalms that ennoble the fallen world where they are heard. Merwin's "state of dispossession, [when] fully recognized, ritualized, and even celebrated" in psalmic intonations, "provides critical leverage against a smugly destructive culture" and affords "momentary glimpses of a world beyond the threshold of ordinary perception," a world promising either annihilation, as in the landscape of *The Lice*, or self-transcendence, as in *The Carrier of Ladders*.[21]

The central riddle of the book, "What we have caught and what we have killed we have left behind, but what has escaped us we bring with us," regarded in the context of "Unfinished Book of Kings," might be interpreted to mean that those prophets who escaped us, those who climbed the cracks in the light, we bring with us into the present, with their blood still on our hands. Death is neither final nor victorious. What the prophets learned for the populace it now has to learn for itself anyway. We drag the ghosts of our dead values and of our martyrs with us everywhere. They accompany us like the "bugs of regret." Spatial distance from the murders provides no psychic distance from them: "So far from the murders / the ruts begin to bleed / but no one hears / our voices" (CL, 58). The farther we move from our deaths, "our voices," the more they pursue us. Death, Merwin says, is a public concern. Disregarded, it becomes a public threat to a self-satisfied nation which refuses to admit death into its consciousness. Like lice,

death is an embarrassing phenomenon for the average American. It is
the prophet's task to make us mindful of its existence and of the existence of higher values than the materialistic values we espouse. In
"Some Last Questions," a question-and-answer poem which precedes
this one in the volume, this sequence of responses is given by a prophetic voice:

> What are the hands
>   A. Paid
> No what are the hands
>   A. Climbing back down the museum wall
>   To their ancestors the extinct shrews that will
>   Have left a message
> What is the silence
>   A. As though it had a right to more
> What are the compatriots
>   A. They make the stars of bone. (L, 6)

These beings, though technically extinct, do not rest: they stir in Merwin's consciousness and in the reader's as he suddenly perceives that
the silence of the extinct animals is *willed* and voluntary ("As though
it had a right to more"). The lines chastise as they instruct: guilt imbues
the knowledge that the stars are made of the bone of extinct creatures.
Bringing the forgotten past to the attention of a callous people is itself
a moral gesture.

Silence becomes positively ominous in "The Wave" where the voice
speaks again: "I inhabit the sound of their pens in boxes / Writing to
the dead" (L, 7). All writing is potentially permeated with this silence:
certainly the poems of *The Lice* are. Gary Thompson says of the language of *The Lice* that it is "even more sparse than in the previous
book. It is as if he no longer needs to describe things in minute detail
because he has become so familiar with them. Within the confines of
the furnace there is little need to differentiate between different types
of birds, stones, trees, animals, windows, etc. He knows them almost as
essences. This gives the poems a primitive, direct tone."[22] Still, the tone
of the lines seems to anticipate indifference or rejection on the part of
the hearer.

Such a rejection is the occasion of "Pieces for Other Lives" (L, 20),
which like many of these poems occurs in the aftermath of the gods'
or extinct animals' departure:

At one stroke out of the ruin
All the watches went out and
The eyes disappeared like martins into their nests
I woke to the slamming of doors and got up naked
The old wind vanished and vanished but was still there
Everyone but the cold was gone for good

And the carol of the miners had just ended. (L, 22)

The setting, situation of the speaker, and mood are reminiscent of the point in the legend of Parsifal where the hero wakes to find himself abandoned by the regal possessors of the Grail Castle for failure to ask the pivotal question or to express concern for the wounded Grail King. Culturally the tenants of the modern world are experiencing a similar abandonment today. The individual is like a sleeper waking to the sight of ruin and the sound of "the slamming of doors . . . / Everyone but the cold was gone for good / And the carol of the miners had just ended." The song of those who dug for the past and made some attempt to treasure the relics of past culture has to get up naked.

In the wake of this departure even "the legends of Accident the hero were marching away down roads that had not been there since the last free election" (L, 14). The hero Accident abandons the unwary, too. All that remains of the prophets are their hunger and the populace's belated discovery "that the bitterness of certain rivers had no source but was caused by their looking for something through the darkness and finding / Something lower" (15). Carol Kyle discusses this scenario of diminishing returns: "The terrible bitterness that occurs to 'certain rivers,' certain streams of the subconscious, belongs to those who are 'looking for something / through the darkness'—the heroes, the idealists, the noblemen. If these distanced figures, these discoverer-poets are subject to find 'Something lower,' that is the risk for kings. And so the poem is a fragmented and unfinished Book of Kings as if there were more to come, as if these scrolls of the Kings had been found in the graves of the Dead Sea.[23] The bitterness of the discoverer-poet is the bitterness of Merwin himself who, writing during the Viet Nam War and in the heyday of the callous ecological destructiveness chronicled in "The Last One" and "For a Coming Extinction," sees the rapaciousness, gullibility, and selfishness of the American.

As for the title, "The Unfinished Book of Kings," the name could be interpreted literally as an indication that the poem chronicles the history of the decline and fall of the United States. The biblical Books of Kings relate the splitting up of the United Kingdoms of Judah and Israel into divided monarchies. The capture and destruction of Jerusalem occurs in Kings, and the fall of both Israel and Judah is interpreted in terms of the Lord's judgment on the disobedient peoples. Through his title Merwin suggests that the modern age parallels the former age: it too is a time when old orders and values are breaking down and are not being replaced by higher values or stronger orders of government.

V *Apocalypse?*

What is man that he should be infinite
W. S. Merwin, "The Gods"

Any contemplation of the images of destruction and the depths of bitterness found in *The Lice* may lead an astute reader to conclude that Merwin is prophesying an apocalypse at hand. Jarold Ramsey addresses himself to this question: "In that primer of modern apocalyptics, *The Sense of an Ending*, Frank Kermode observes how the experience of *déja vu* seems naturally to attend meditations on The End—an observation pertinent to Merwin's vision. The imagination baffled at its impulse to conceive images of a post-apocalyptic future becomes suffused with an uncanny sense that what is happening has all happened before."[24] It is this mentality that impels Merwin to write a poem "For the Anniversary of my Death" which opens "Every year without knowing it I have passed the day / When the last fires will wave to me / And the silence will set out / Tireless traveller / Like the beam of a lightless star" (L, 58). The "lightless star" is a constant image for any event whose significance he cannot fully fathom. Mystery and unfathomability also characterize the experience of *déjà vu:* one senses that something has occurred before but one cannot account for how, when, or why.

In fact, the mood, voice, and locus of *The Lice* are themselves *déjà vus;* all have appeared before in "Canso," published in 1954:

I will myself become
A Hades into which I can descend.

It will be a domain of déjà-vus,
The final most outlandish fastness of

Familiarity without memory,
Whose set dimensions, whose mode of privacy
And mode of pain I with my living breath
Shall enter, saying, "Like an Icarus
I have fallen into my shadow." There shall be seen
The death of the body walking in shapes of bodies
Departure's self hid in a guise of sojourn,
As it seems among the living. But on those hills
The shadows of sheep are folded, not the sheep
But on those lakes or the mirages of
Those lakes not birds are reflected, but the flight
Of birds across no sky. It is nevertheless
A place of recognition, though it be
Of recognition of nothing; a place of knowledge
Though it be knowledge of nothing; in this land
No landscape but a demeanor of distance
Where interchangeably the poles are death
And death, as in an opposition of mirrors
Where no beginning is, no end, I have lived
Not recognizing, for as long as knowledge. (F, 114–15)

These stanzas define the limits of the Hades of the self "into which I can descend"—into which he *does* descend in *The Lice*. There the polarity between death and death creates a static, bodiless region where no substance, only shadow and mirage exist: "Departure's self hid in the guise of sojourn." If the speaker is Icarus, he represents fallen ambition. Death mirroring death in timeless recognition provokes a "Familiarity without memory, / Whose set dimensions, whose mode of privacy / And mode of pain I . . . Shall enter." The world of *The Lice* is a private and painful hell: the cardinal experience is intimate "familiarity without memory," an experience those in Dante's *Inferno* testify to in their own "domain of déjà-vus." Although literally this is Hades, it might just as well be an image of the end of time, the apocalyptic diminishment T. S. Eliot records in *The Hollow Men:* "This is the way the world ends / Not with a bang but a whimper."

The lice or "bugs of regret" which live off the ghostly presences inhabiting this world could be the prior life's "unresolved alternatives, the frustrated purposes, the guilt, missed chances, the unwritten poems of his discontinuous lives."[25] To name an entity gives one ineluctable power over it, yet none of these entities is precisely named or nameable by the speaker. As demonstrated earlier regarding the poem "The Animals," the first poem in *The Lice,* when "I with no voice" can

remember "names to invent for them," one may be won over and
return. Until the speaker can name it, its status will stay unresolved
and he will bring it along with him into the present and future. What
one cannot name one cannot stand on equal footing with; it stays latent
in the subconscious, it continues to bear witness to failure. Ghosts speak
only when proffered the blood of remorse or grief:

> New ghost is that what you are
> Standing on the stairs of water
>
> No longer surprised
>
> Hope and grief are still our wings
> Why we cannot fly
>
> What failure still keeps you
> Among us the unfinished

So opens the poem "Is That What You Are," the second poem in
The Lice. Note that in the seventh line "we" are the "unfinished," not
the ghost. And by implication, the "failure" mentioned in the line
before is "ours" not his. Proof of this resides in the speaker's query and
response: "Why are you there / I did not think I had anything else to
give / The wheels say it after me." His weariness and sadness are
apparent here. What we have missed resides with us in our houses and
is all about us, riding on the very air we breathe. We look through it
while "Standing on the stairs of water" or looking out the window each
morning. Strange personages of whose existence we slowly become
aware enter our rooms unsummoned: in an earlier poem "Witnesses"
evening enters this way and "bats flower in the crevices / You and
your brothers" (MT, 44). In "Evening" Merwin writes, "I look up but
it is only / Evening again the old hat without a head / How long will
it be till he speaks when he passes" (L, 51). They do not speak, and he
cannot find the words to address them. Despair has moved in for good,
and it clings, becoming a familiar inhabitant.

The dead do not question the futility of their lives, so why should
the poet? In the outstanding poem "A Scale in May," he says:

> Through the day the nameless stars keep passing the door
> That have come all the way out of death
> Without questions

The walls of light shudder and an owl wakes in the heart
I cannot call upon words
The sun goes away to set elsewhere

Before nightfall colorless petals blow under the door
And the shadows
Recall their ancestors in the house beyond death. (L, 50)

"I cannot call upon words" sums up the entire experience of *The Lice*.
A penetrating wordless horror causes the light to shudder, "an owl
wakes in the heart / . . . The sun goes away to set elsewhere." And this
"is the time when the beards of the dead get their growth." What
recourse is there? A shocking knife image concludes "Is That What
You Are," a symbol of deliverance and also danger: "And at the windows in the knives / You are watching." Knives are instruments of
death as well as self-knowledge, probing insight as well as self-destruc-
tion. Seeing into the mirror they provide, seeing through their "watching" eyes may enable the speaker to penetrate the obscurity of the self
and find then the words "to invent for them." He may seize the oppor-
tunity to communicate with these ghosts and dispel them by eliminat-
ing their reason for existence. "Hope and grief are still our wings," but
"why we cannot fly" he does not know. Though "I did not think I had
anything else to give," to find what he has to give would be to solve
the riddle of the lice, and thus to achieve self-transcendence. As one of
the sayings of Antonio Porchia that Merwin was translating around this
time goes: "No one understands that you have given everything. You
must give more."[26] Without the cleaving potential of the knife his frozen consciousness can only "remember that I am falling / That I am
the reason / And that my words are the garment of what I shall never
be / Like the tucked sleeve of a one-armed boy."

A final experience of *déjà vu* in the last lines of the book confirms
the saving potential of recognition, remembrance, and waking to the
call of the present:

In the dark while the rain fell
The gold chanterelles pushed through a sleep that was not mine

Waking me
So that I came up the mountain to find them
Where they appear it seems I have been before
I recognize their haunts as though remembering
Another life

> Where else am I walking even now
> Looking for me

If lives are exchangeable, so are griefs. If "I" can be walking experiencing "their haunts as though remembering / Another life," another "I" could be walking "Looking for me." This poignant process wakes the seeker of "gold chanterelles" up from his bed of ash. He rises and walks and is healed.

In a critical discussion of the future of poetry, published in *The Distinctive Voice* (1966), Merwin asserts that poetry is now facing extinction just as certainly as the pupfish or any of the vanishing species: "But then, among my peculiar failings is an inability to believe that the experience of being human, that gave rise to the arts in the first place, can continue to be nourished in a world contrived and populated by nothing but humans."[27] He fears that poetry itself may be merely vestigial or atavistic in an age when our lives are lived wholly apart from animals and our kinship with other forms of life is attenuated or nonexistent; thus it is fitting, that in "Looking for Mushrooms at Sunrise," the non-human world ventures into his consciousness, warns him, rouses him:

> When it is not yet day
> I am walking on centuries of dead chestnut leaves
> In a place without grief
> Though the oriole
> Out of another life warns me
> That I am awake (L, 80)

He perceives a voice "Out of another life" while "walking on centuries of dead chestnut leaves." The leaves, symbols of the eternal recycling and recurrence of lives, participate in communication with him like the oriole who warns him out of another life "That I am awake." The leaves dispel grief, pointing as they do to the potential of other existences for the poet. Heightened awareness of other dimensions in our own lives and consciousnesses derives from close attention to nature. Lives as simple as those of the "gold chanterelles" can push through one's sleep and impel one to "recognize their haunts as though remembering / Another life." To remain open to such experience, Merwin implies, is to draw on the resources and strengths of former—and even future—lives; this seems all the more necessary in a fallen, disrupted time.

The poem ends in acute awareness that another higher self is "walking even now / Looking for me." Does despair prompt him to rationalize the existence of another "I" who searches for him? Or is the ending merely an exquisite aesthetic flourish, a gesture to make the poem "work"? A quantity of evidence drawn from his next three books of poetry, *The Carrier of Ladders*, *Writings to an Unfinished Accompaniment*, and *The Compass Flower*, substantiates the fact that in the 1970s Merwin was newly receptive to other dimensions of consciousness, other non-human voices in nature, and other ways of perceiving the life cycle. In "Words from a Totem Animal" in *The Carrier of Ladders*, he writes, "Send me out into another life / lord because this one is growing faint / I do not think it goes all the way" (19).

Merwin mourns the fact that today poetry and the animals are being relegated to an inferior position. For him they embody a dimension of spiritual life that is being lost: both are like "that Biblical waif . . . the spirit. No one has any claims on it, no one deserves it, no one knows where it goes. It is not pain, and it is not the subconscious, though it can hail from either as though it were at home there." In order to keep the spirit alive, despite difficult, even desperate times, he will continue to write, for "absolute despair has no art, and I imagine the writing of a poem, in whatever mode, still betrays the existence of hope, which is why poetry is more and more chary of the conscious mind, in our age." The reflection of conscious mind can only lead him to despair: rational, logical examination of history militates against his feeling any hope for the future. Still, he asserts, "what the poem manages to find hope for may be part of what it keeps trying to say."[28] What Merwin said of the small bird in "The Room" might be said of the spirit and voice of *The Lice:* "You would say it was dying it is immortal."

CHAPTER 5

Ecologist of the Word and World

*T*HE *Carrier of Ladders,* awarded the Pulitzer Prize in 1971, is a
book of retrenchment, reassessment, but not, like *The Lice,* a book
of bitter regret or alienation. In *The Carrier of Ladders,* W. S. Merwin
has reexamined the stylistic and personal choices he made in the 1960s,
but he continues speaking from the core of the self, exploring the core
of the furnace.

Ladders are tools for ascending: his poetry of the 1970s sustains a
quiet ascendancy over the political, moral, and social concerns that
plagued him in *The Lice.* In this book and the two succeeding volumes
of poetry, *Writings to an Unfinished Accompaniment* (1973) and *The
Compass Flower* (1977), Merwin joins Octavio Paz in affirming that
"Poetry is an entry into being."[1] His mood and approach are best
expressed by the writer of a sacred Indian poem he translated during
this period:

> I am climbing
> everywhere is
>
> coming up

I   Innocence and Affirmation

In his "Prayer for my Daughter," W. B. Yeats envisions a soul that
drives "all hatred . . . hence" and recovers "radical innocence." Such
is the soul that animates W. S. Merwin's poetry of the 1970s. A spirit
of innocence, a fresh, wondering approach to all aspects of nature, pre-
vails in these books. Confident of his location in the universe and in the
poem, Merwin feels no need to fill in all the spaces or all the silences.
A spirit of letting be or letting go as well as a sense of freedom pre-
dominate. Also readily discernible is a preoccupation with beginnings.
Denis Donoghue has observed that "*The Carrier of Ladders* . . . begins

with poems about beginnings, implying rock bottom starting out again."[2] In "The Piper" Merwin broaches the subject of his growth "backward" into innocence:

> It has taken me till now
> to be able to say
> even this
> it has taken me this long
> to know what I cannot say
> where it begins
> like the names of the hungry
>
> Beginning
> I am here
> please
> be ready to teach me
> I am almost ready to learn (CL, 28–9)

In this poem he names his muse the piper and speaks of sitting "high above" him "but hearing him / once / and never moving from my book / and the narrow / house full of pregnant women." Unlike the Pied Piper, his muse was not successful in leading away the child in him. He has wanted to be delivered into freedom, to move "from my book" before this, but the constraints of conformity or decorum have inhibited his muse-in-waiting. He assesses his mood and poetic mode at the time: "I was older then / than I hope ever to be again / that summer sweating in the attic / in the foreign country."

Seen from the vantage point of a more recent poetry Merwin's poetic corpus traces a progress from experience to an innocence that is the culmination of the longest, richest experience. It records the progress from constriction and despair to nascent hope. Even *The Lice* has at least one poem hinting at reevaluation. In "The Child," old standards and values are being reexamined: "I pass skins withering in gardens / that I see now are not familiar" (L, 37). There is a recognition and admission of old mistakes, a sense that his old premises are being shed like withered skins and that new ones will soon take their place. The last lines of "The Child" present a view of memory new in Merwin's poetry:

> This silence coming at intervals out of the shell of names
> It must be all one person really coming at

Different hours for the same thing
If I could learn the word for yes it could teach me questions
I would see that it was itself every time and I would
Remember to say take it up like a hand
And go with it this is at last
Yourself

The child that will lead you (L, 38)

Echoing Isaiah (11:6), Merwin asserts his need for a recovery of simple childlike confidence, a simple faith in and knowledge of his own feelings. David H. Zucker's review of *Writings to an Unfinished Accompaniment* is appropriately entitled "In Search of the Simplicities."[3] That is the theme of these three books—a search for an affirmation of the value of poetic and personal simplicity, innocence, and communion with nature.

Strength and salvation come from attending to the message from within oneself and remembering to recognize "This silence" as "The child that will lead you" beside the still waters of peace and self-knowledge. The self-reflective memory, properly used, can bring one into a fuller affirmation of one's own identity and of life: "If I could learn the word for yes it could teach me questions / I would see that it was itself every time and I would / Remember to say take it up like a hand / And go with it." Memory can connect the rememberer with the best and most innocent "child" part of himself. "The child that will lead you," like the holy animals and saints discussed in Chapter 2, has a wisdom beyond the limits of rational or logical knowledge and, more important, it resides within each person. And what better guide is there for *puer aeternis* than a child? Merwin's restless seeking sustains his imagination; his poetry depicts youthful subjects—young horses, blossoms, "the year still a child" (CL, 9).

The sequence of poems in *The Carrier of Ladders* describes the arc of the seasons running from spring to spring. If, as Richard Wilbur says, "The work of every good poet may be seen in one way as an exploration and declaration of the self,"[4] then these books—particularly *The Carrier of Ladders*—can be understood as Merwin's declaration of his own youth and, by extension, his youthful self. Paradoxically, he is now so far from having to declare his independence that he has earned his right to exist happily as a child. He sees now that his former poetic selves are "withered skins" which are "not familiar." In a poem called "The Removal" he explains "the soles of our feet are black stars / but ours is the theme of the light." In another poem he reveals an inner mandate: "In front of me it is written / *This is the end of the past / Be happy.*"

Each poem in these volumes renders a moment of natural awareness. The voice speaks directly, clearly, gently, simply. There is in these lines the child's natural acceptance of his friends; animals, birds, other people are cordially invited into the poem to share in the pervading natural awareness of reality. Although the setting is the natural setting of "Avoiding News by the River," now the poet avoids no one. Far from the podiums for public address or the majesty of presidents, he is still acutely aware of American political reality, yet detached from it. He has come to the end of a long, complex process of evolution from "I believe, therefore I am" through "I fear I am forever I am / fear I am alone I fear I am" (CL, 85) to "I affirm, therefore I am" unto "the uttermost parts of aye" (CL, 85). He has found a sure, secure identity, that of the wondering *puer aeternis*. He appears to be saying that "the only hope is to begin again with a recovered ABC of feeling."[5] Relinquishing the past, he turns his gaze toward the future. Speaking of a stone, he says, "The eyes are not yet made that can see it" (CL, 124). As this line indicates, the gaze is now prophetic. He assumes an ecclesiastical tone in "Midnight in Early Spring":

> some alien blessing
> is on its way to us
> some prayer ignored for centuries
> is about to be granted to the prayerless
> in this place
> who were you
> cold voice born in captivity
> rising
> last martyr of a hope
> last word of a language
> last son
> other half of grief
> who were you
>
> so that we may know why
> when the streams
> wake tomorrow and we are free (CL, 75)

The streams of creativity are waking throughout *The Carrier of Ladders* and flowing in outstanding poetry by one who is himself "last martyr of a hope / last word of a language / last son / other half of grief." Having discovered freedom and youth at last, he has discovered who he is.

II   *The Animals Come Down from the Mountains*

Between publication of *The Lice* and *The Carrier of Ladders*, Merwin was finding his native assurance, relocating at the center, and preparing to start anew. Two poems from *Writings to an Unfinished Accompaniment* will serve to illustrate the new openness and the childlike sensibility he now displays. In "Notes for a Preface" he said that the poet employs "What gifts he can muster . . . to call the next real creature from the ark."[6] In the poem "Animals from Mountains," "The child that will lead you" summons many of these "real creatures from the ark":

> When I was small and stayed quiet
> some animals came
> new ones each time
> and waited there near me
> and all night they were eating the black
>
> they knew me they knew me
> nobody saw them
> I watched how they watched me
> they waited right there
> nobody heard them talking laughing
> laughing
> Laugh they told me nobody will hear (W, 52.)

The self-assuring repetition of "they knew me" suggests the child's repeating words to himself alone in the dark where "they were eating the black." The secret camaraderie of animals and the child has the status of a special community: it is the nighttime communion of the child with dream animals. The language the child speaks with the animals who visit him privately is "the original idiom, . . . a tongue loosed in service of immediate recognitions."[7] Or, as Emerson expressed it; it is language "in its infancy, when it is all poetry."[8]

Merwin's "Animals from Mountains" ends: "but the mountain's gone / and some of us / never came back all the way"—the poet is definitely one "of us." He has said that it is impossible for him to imag-

ine the continuation of the human race in a world populated by nothing but humans; therefore, as an adult he searches for the names or
words these animals will understand, the better to give "utterance to
the unutterable experience of being alive, and consciously mortal, and
human."[9] To retain a strong sense of being human he must literally
keep up his animal spirits. Merwin's "The Day" personifies the day as
a creature who can be awakened by "your" calling; here is the entire
poem:

> If you could take the day by the hand
> even now and say Come Father
> calling it by your own name
> it might rise in its blindness with all
> its knuckles and curtains
> and open the eyes it was born with (W, 14)

The child's awareness of other existences or realities unfathomable
by adults is invoked again in "Snowfall," which he dedicates to his
mother:

> I see that the silent kin I loved as a child
> have arrived all together in the night
> from the old country
> they remembered
> and everything remembers (CL, 69)

These kin who "remembered" would at first seem to be creatures
like the "Animals from Mountains" but turn out to be snow, which he
consumes joyously in lines that recall his "eating the silence of animals"
in "Whenever I Go There": "I eat from the hands / of what for years
have been junipers / the taste has not changed / I am beginning /
again." Here the taste of snow becomes "The child that will lead me"
back to beginnings. Memory returns him to his true self.

In the more innocent poetry in open forms of *The Carrier of Ladders, Writings to an Unfinished Accompaniment,* and *The Compass
Flower,* the openness is integrated with the style: there is less verbal
self-consciousness and a more rooted, realistic consciousness of self. The
spare, stark style of the three books complements their condensed
utterance. Certainly some poems still treat the alienation and disillu-
sionment, burdens, and trouble that the book's epigraph proclaims, yet
a fresh wind blows through many of the poems. A spirit of openness to

new experience and a childlike hopefulness pervades much of the poetry. Here Merwin can merge with nature, affirming his brotherhood with it. Here for the first time he acknowledges and praises the uniqueness and separateness of natural lives and existences. He writes of nature out of sheer love for it. For Merwin nature is no longer merely a symbol of simplicity, innocence, and intelligence with which to contrast man's treachery and inanity, as it had been in "Avoiding News by the River" where he could say "If I was not human I would not be ashamed of anything" (L, 71). Instead he now loves each discrete natural object or creature in its own right and on its own merits. "The silence and solitude . . . of nature can be pregnant with the news of some other world beyond destructions of this one. Although such a world can never be fully revealed or understood, it can be glimpsed by a speaker who respects its invisibility. . . ."[10] From visible and invisible aspects of nature he receives a renewed moral vitality of the sort projected in the last poem of *The Lice*. On the strength of this new vitality, he plumbs the depths of his private self, getting to know a child-self for the first time.

Self-revelation has always been extremely difficult for Merwin, the intensely private person who writes, "I am the son of fear though I find out for myself" (CL, 92). Even in *The Carrier of Ladders* poems like "The Owl" (5) reflect the pain of personal revelation. Here he *is* the shy, reserved owl: "I retreat before / your question as before my own / through branches who / am I hiding?" This expression of the pain of "opening up" is symptomatic of the imminence of change. Yet it would also seem that concealment is one condition of the poet's calling, although occasionally the poet himself even questions the necessity for hiding: "what creature in the bowels quaking / that should not be raised / against the night / crying its truth at last." In fact, the speaker is always questioning. Many of his questions emanate from a strong sense of his own morality, his sense of himself as having no more durability than "a spine of smoke in the forest."

Alan Williamson writes that Merwin's sensibility is "rather ethereal, and, like Northrop Frye's or Robert Graves', finds its music in the apprehension of orderly ritual patterns behind all temporal events."[11] These "orderly ritual patterns," cadences and repetitions of word, thought, and phrase, bind poems together harmoniously. They create poetry that is lyrically and imaginatively pure. The line is correspondingly clean and free of encumbrances. There is a lyrical formality in all but the most recent poetry.

Of the importance of cadence in Merwin's poetry, Denis Donoghue declares, "Mr. Merwin does by cadence what other poets do by image and figure, the further difference being that cadence is the last part of words to go and best part to start from."[12] Its cadence is one noticeable aspect of the recent poetry and may indeed be "the best part to start from" when beginning to read Merwin. Merwin works rhythmically through each poem, letting the reader follow the musical ebb and flow of his thought: each Merwin poem has a rhythmic integrity, preserved through incremental repetition as well as through rhymes of thought. This integrity is part of his uniqueness as a poet.

Another part of his uniqueness is his kinship with the transcendent. Referring to a poem entitled "The Cuckoo Myth," Slowik says, "Like Shelley's skylark, Keats' nightingale and Wordsworth's cuckoo (in 'To the Cuckoo') the cuckoo of 'Cuckoo Myth' [CL, 97–8] seems to have some contact with a transcendent time and place. While constrained to a time, . . . she can fly beyond time to an integral and absolute time, a place of origins: 'the first season . . . the undivided . . . the unturning.' She returns as bearer of light and love."[13] Since man fell from grace through his engagement in natural creation, it is through natural creation he can be saved. Though Merwin cherishes individual trees, lakes, and animals, he knows it is the hidden part of each creature or natural object that partakes of the other world, the transcendent world. From contact with that "transcendent time and place," the creature becomes a "bearer of light and love." And the cuckoo of the myth is "she / that from hiding sings / from dark coverts / from gates where ghosts / stand open."

Metaphorically speaking, Merwin's gods are now manifest in all aspects of natural creation. They grace nature with their presence even as they inform it with significance and meaning. He happens upon a little horse "from some other forest" and addresses it worshipfully: "I would have wished for you if I had known" (CL, 54). Knowing it brings about personal fulfillment for him: "what a long time the place was empty / . . . I could not have told what was missing / . . . I hope you will come with me to where I stand / . . . by the patient water / that has no father nor mother." To see into life and meaning in nature, the poet only needs to "open the eyes [he] was born with," look about him, and name what he sees, written in lines which are "a resonance echoing no sound." His mere presence in nature summons the "next real creature from the ark."

In *The Moving Target* he was already subliminally aware that his search would be a journey from experience into innocence: in "The Present" he confesses "when what I am trying to find is / The beginning, / In the ashes" (51). For Merwin charity can only begin in the internal world of the self; from there it moves to an affirmation of lives and existences outside his own. He can express private emotions of charity for other beings but can hardly express a public love for his country.

In the last poem of *The Moving Target* he wrote that "An open doorway / Speaks for me / Again" (97). With that statement his words become departures; they open onto the world beyond perception and consciousness. The lines keep on making the "difficult journey of detachment from and yet commitment to the world."[14] But only in *The Carrier of Ladders* and the later books of poetry does he actually "come home" in spirit and embrace charity.

If America's public secularization of spirit has resulted in the diminishment of human beings, hope and wisdom reside in beginning again on one's own terms and in conserving what resources of mind, body, and spirit one has left. In one of the first poems of *The Carrier of Ladders* Merwin writes "and what is wisdom if it is not / now / in the loss that has not left this place" (8). Here the positive is conceived in negative terms as "the loss that has not left this place."

III *Oneness and Identity*

In Merwin's poetry of the 1970s the search for oneness and communion with other aspects of nature is conceived positively, but the search for identity is described in negatives, circumscribed by negations. In his perception, identity is often associated with division: awareness of identity necessitates an awareness of division from an original harmony and union. He believes that integrity, oneness of self and spirit, is being undermined as it is undervalued in the technological age. "Where there is no vision, the people perish": American civilization today attests to the fact that mind and will are perishing. The fragmentation is poignantly imaged in this sequence of lines from "Plane":

> I imagine the deities come and go
> without departures

> and with my mind infinitely divided and hopeless
> like a stockyard seen from above
> and my will like a withered body muffled
> in qualifications until it has no shape
> I bleed in my place (CL, 3)

This "I" is like the "I" of "The Owl"; a universal voice speaks here, and we sense that it is not merely of his own personal mental divisions or of his own personal will "muffled / in qualifications" that he is speaking.

Following the line "I bleed in my place" comes these lines: "where is no vision of the essential nakedness of the gods / nor of that / nakedness / the seamless garment of heaven" (3). Although clinging to "the nuclear identity of a personality" might constitute in these changing times "peculiar psychic greed,"[15] still to be able to integrate mind and will would, at the very least, eliminate psychic pain and possibly even ensure some "vision of the essential nakedness of the gods" or of "that / nakedness / the seamless garment of heaven." In his present divided state, however, man has no vision of this or "any other / nakedness." He is like a plane departing from this life: "We hurtle forward and seem to rise." The rising is only apparent: it only "seems" to occur while he bleeds in his assigned place. Richard Howard summarizes this negative pole of *The Carrier of Ladders* when he says of the poems, "what they are developing toward . . . is a quality of life that used to be called visionary, and which must be characterized by its negatives, by what it is not, for what it is cannot be spoken."[16] And, one might add, the vision they are seeking cannot yet be seen on earth. Today's world is a world where logical constructs have "reduced reality to a hand-list of trivia."[17] The essential nakedness of the gods is a vision for the first and last ages of mankind but not for this age.

If the mind and will are "muffled" and no vision comes, clear-cut decisions, valiant acts of attention are impossible. Inner awareness of division paralyzes any quest for a unique identity or individuality. How else to express these limitations, even in the midst of prosperity, but in negations?

At the same time that Merwin's poetry records the seismic shocks of fragmenting identity, it achieves unprecedented purity while aspiring to a realm of oneness where "the light is not yet / divided" (CL, 123). The poetry reaches into a time before God created heaven and earth when all was still primordial unity. Since division did not yet exist, hope and the will are also undivided: it is still possible to hope whole-heartedly and genuinely. Even though "it is a long way / to the first / anything" (123), the poet *can* conceive of making the journey with an undivided mind and will.

In *The Carrier of Ladders* and the succeeding books, a search for oneness becomes a search for integrity, clarity of vision: "I go eating nothing so you will be one and clear" (CL, 39). Oneness is not always associated with the past. In "Words from a Totem Animal" he conjectures:

> Maybe I will come
> to where I am one
> and find
> I have been waiting there
> as a new
> year finds the song of the nuthatch (CL, 19)

Here the line break after "new" emphasizes the association between oneness, integration of identity, and the future. Wholeness is forecast. Evan Watkins notes, "The movement of identity cancels all doubleness and division in the reification of its own source as a goal."

IV   *The Mind in Nature*

"Now it is Clear" from *The Carrier of Ladders* is a recognition and affirmation of the poet's identity as wanderer: "Now it is clear to me that no roots are mine / . . . and the forest will know it / we will both know it" (109). That he and the forest both know it is what is important to him. At other times, he experiences a kinship or is aware of a presence whose identity he slowly discerns: "I shake you in your heavy sleep / then the sun comes / and I see you are one of the stones" (CL, 39).

This mutual knowing also implies a less static relationship between the mind and its materials than existed in the past. What Denis Donoghue wrote of *The Lice* is equally applicable here: "Mr. Merwin's poetry is not, then, modern, in Barthes' stringent sense: he is still looking for a natural syntax in which relations between one thing and another are given; to be discovered, not imposed by will or whim. When he turns from 'objects solitary and terrible' it is always to look for a sign, something to live by. Perhaps the objects are still a code, however secret; if so, it may still be possible to break it. Emblems of fulfillment include, in the recent poems, maps, names, stars, song, trumpet, flag, the instinct by which streams find one another."[19] One who approaches the poetry with patience *can* break the code; but he must realize that the poet himself is engaged in a constantly evolving process of recognition of signs, hence the code changes as his own deciphering and his modes of perception change. Poems are often named for objects in Merwin's work because each poem is itself a deciphering of "natural syntax [the syntax of *nature*] in which relations between one thing and another are given." An object's significance lies latent in nature until the astute poet/discoverer happens onto it and suddenly *sees;* each poem is a seeing-into-the-depths of an object or a being. For instance, "Tool" starts with a definition: "If it's invented it will be used" (W, 26).

In his comments on his poetry for a dictionary of authors, Merwin says: "Writing is something I know little about; less at some times than at others. I think, though, that so far as it is poetry it is a matter of correspondences: one glimpses them, pieces of an order, or thinks one does, and tries to convey the sense of what one has seen to those to whom it may matter including, if possible, one's self."[20] Merwin speaks of the discipline of seeing these relationships that unlock perception elsewhere in *Writings to an Unfinished Accompaniment,* a book whose very title reflects the evolving character of his code: "and in the dream / for every real lock / there is only one real key / . . . it's the key to the one real door / . . . and I am saying to the hand / turn / open the river" (66). The hand turning "the one real key" "to the one real door" not only opens the doors of perception, it will unleash the flood as well.

V   *Time and Poetic Form*

Merwin's *The Carrier of Ladders, Writings to an Unfinished Accompaniment*, and *The Compass Flower* are attempts to impart the knowledge of the interior that he promised in *The Drunk in the Furnace*. One basic theme of *Writings to an Unfinished Accompaniment* is "time, upon which we have based our language, logic, history, and indeed, the entire way we see our world." By banishing sequential or temporal order from the poem and casting each poem in spatial form, he is "able to show us ourselves and our world in a fresh new way. Perhaps we see it for the first time."[21]

The British critic Robert Shaw comments on Merwin's spatial form: "He makes history spatial and travels through it as though it were an alternative geography on a plane with the present physical order."[22] This dislocation of chronology and this space travel annihilating time are not the acts of one who has no knowledge of history. On the contrary, *The Lice* and the books of prose are permeated by a keener cognizance of history and its implications for the present age. In fact, only by disorienting time-bound facts and thereby effecting the illusion of timelessness can he crash through the light barrier into transcendence of a time consciousness which today we have "too much with us."

He writes, "The visitation that is going to be a poem finds the form it needs" (O, 279). And this form contains "the time of the poem, the time in which it was written, and the sense of recurrence in which the unique moment of vision was set" (O, 277). But further on in the same essay "On Open Form," which was first published shortly after the publication of *The Carrier of Ladders,* he relates the discovery of the stanza by the troubadours. In the Middle Ages, he says, form seemed "transparent" because both "the role of time in the poem and the role of the poem in time doubtless seemed clear and simple" to the great master of the art; today, however, form may indeed be "mere confection." Merwin writes, "For us, for whom everything is in question, the making [of poetry] keeps leading us back into the patterns of a world of artifice so intricate, so insidious, and so impressive, that often it seems indistinguishable from the whole of time" (O, 277). This comment reveals that his is a strikingly medieval view of time: time the devourer works insidiously to absorb one wholly in the "inescapably technical" to the point that life is exhausted before one can be conscious of its passage. Still, he would never advise that one be either unduly aware of or oblivious to time. His poems move beyond time; like the cuckoo in "Cuckoo Myth" they fly "beyond time to an integral and absolute time, a place of origins."[23] Moreover, as Malkoff points out, "Viewing time *sub specie aeternitatis,* granting equal reality to time future as is granted to time present and time past, Merwin labels the linear sense of time—that is, time as inexorable, unfolding, continual movement—as illusory."[24] Therefore, although he does fear poetry's passing away in time, his ultimate view of time in the individual poem is of a time present, past, and future all merging into the eternal and effecting an escape into timelessness.[25]

Merwin conceives of history as "the form of despair reserved for the living" (MP, 146). To dwell on history is to yield to despair. On the other hand, to yield to a euphoria over past accomplishments is equally inadvisable: Merwin warns, "Our age pesters us with the illusion that we have realized a great deal. The agitation serves chiefly to obscure what we have forgotten, into whose limbo poetry itself at times seems about to pass" (O, 278). The most constructive action we can take is to continue creating, bringing new words and beings to life: "it seems as though what is needed to make a poem . . . is . . . an unduplicatable resonance, something that would be like an echo except that it is repeating no sound. Something that always belonged to it: its sense and its conformation before it entered words" (O, 278). And, one could add, before it entered the world. The last sentence gives a mystical dimension to the resonance a poem strains to capture. Because this resonance is so fragile, composed partially of silence, its "setting down" or form must itself be nearly transparent. In the recent books of poetry, Merwin has fully accepted the silence of his new voice. Gary Thompson explains, "He no longer finds it absolutely necessary to explain where he is and how he works" in his poetry. "Instead he moves from one corner to the next quietly pointing out things we might miss."[26]

Because composing out of and in silence is such a tenuous process, he is naturally wary of "technique" which might come to "encroach on" or "doctor the source." He writes, "It is love, I imagine, more than learning, that may eventually make it possible to be aware of the living resonance before it has words" (ST, vii). An arbitrarily imposed form is antithetical to the creative force he calls "love": left unwatched, form could become a "deftness usurping the authority it was reared to serve."

Mary Helen Slowik, who contends that "Merwin would be a central figure" in any study of "the evolution of poetic form in the mid-twentieth century," comments on his statements on form thus: "Note that the 'source' and 'authority' reside in the 'living resonance before it has words.' It is this preverbal dimension that paradoxically informs Merwin's definition of poetic form: 'A poetic form: the setting down of a way of hearing how poetry happens in words. The words themselves do not make it.'"[27] Poems, like "silence" in "The Child," come to him "at intervals out of the shell of names" (L, 38). His poet's ear and sensitivity is the child that will lead him.

Through immersing himself in silence, Merwin learns to hear more clearly. Through close attention to the preverbal resonance he attains a closer poetic approximation of its form before it entered words, and this attentiveness justifies his existence as a poet. The "pieces of an order" he glimpses fulfill his mission.

Silence is the hallmark of the poetry, a phenomenon even more central to his poetry than time. Here more than ever before "Silence is my shepherd" (CL, 116). In "Words from a Totem Animal," the totem animal addresses his god, "oh god of beginnings / immortal": "I know your silence / and the repetition / like that of a word in the ear of death / teaching / itself / itself" (CL, 15). The silence is attempting to teach the totem animal, although at present it is only teaching itself. Any unsoundable mystery is conceived as silence, as the hulk of a dead ship is in "The Hulk":

> It must be named for silence
> the iron whale asleep on its side
> in the breathless port
> a name rusted out
> in an unknown
> unknown language (CL, 82)

What better metaphor for silence than "an unknown / unknown language"? In communing with the silence, the mystery of life, he finds confidence and mystical knowledge. He turns the key and opens the river. Then "Silent rivers / fall toward us / without explaining" (CL, 117).

VI   Recent Poetry: The Retreat from the Word

> at the end
> birds lead something down to me
> it is silence

In many ways Merwin's style in *The Carrier of Ladders, Writings to an Unfinished Accompaniment,* and *The Compass Flower* resemble his style in the two previous books. The new style has evolved through metamorphosis rather than through a process of stripping away; it has come about through an internal evolution that stands revealed in the poetry. Though the careful reader will discern an occasional reemergence of the thought and themes of the early poetry as well as its basic cadences, essentially this poetry exists in a "naked condition, where it touches on all that is unrealized" (O, 278). In the latest volumes of poetry, one can observe the breakdown of grammar—or a liberation from it. One finds a diction of division and affirmation, more one-word lines and shorter lines generally, no punctuation. The line breaks are never syntactical or grammatical breaks; lines are broken after significant words or bizarre images. Paradox, reversal, and a quiet intensity of tone force the reader to participate actively in deciphering the poem's developing meaning.

The unexpected breaks create intensity, but they also fragment the thread of thought, splitting poems into poem sequences. Examples of this phenomenon are "The Black Plateau" and "Words from a Totem Animal" (CL, 39–41, 15–19). This style accommodates itself well to a rendering of dissolution of the self and of traditional orders. The impetus here is justification—largely self-justification—and self-analysis. Because he explores not the secure but the fragmented self, often on the brink of renewal, a disparity of images and alternative disciplines congregate in the poetry. His transcendent imagination treats "geography history law comedy / fear law poetry major prophets / minor prophets that pass in the night / it is a mother and guiding light" (CL, 85). The "it" referred to here is the imagination in touch with self and silence.

If "it is the edges of things / the light of things" that he touches on in his poetry, "logic follows but I advance in / everything and so discovery" (CL, 85). Revelation and discovery are reached when one breaks the logic barrier and tests the outer boundaries of consciousness. Emerson insisted in "The Poet" that "The condition of true naming, on the poet's part, is resigning himself to the divine *aura* which breathes through all forms." Such a Transcendentalist view is not alien to Merwin's own view of the imagination. His metaphor for the transcendent poetic voice is the cuckoo who

> flew again to the first season
> to the undivided
> returned from there bringing Love
> a light for the unhappy
> but the light bore with it
> its hiding (CL, 97)

It retreats "before your question" and is ambiguous. What the poet discovers when the divine aura breathes through him will be "Love" which he hands over to his readers; but the writing is cryptic and contains "its hiding."

Love and something akin to a "divine aura" imbues the most recent

poetry. In *The Compass Flower* his neo-Descartesian formula is
altered to read "I love, therefore I am." This is especially observable
in "Kore" (49–56), "The Morning," "Summer Doorway," "Islands,"
and "Mountain Day" (61–65), all written for Dana Naone, to whom
the book is dedicated. Merwin has come full circle back to his vantage
point in 1956, when he wrote, "The impulse of a poem, of any body-
ing-forth, must be love in *some* sort, and there is the mystery."[28] Merwin still sees love as infinite, logic as finite. If logic sets boundaries and
restricts possibilities, he bursts the boundaries to explore off-limits possibilities. He opens up his style to encompass a logic in the lines,
between the lines. He opens himself to all potentials in life and in art.
Rivers and water are his symbols for the plentitude of the imagination
and imaginative transcendence.

The language of Merwin's poetry has completed its levelling process:
it is wholly the language of a man living easily with himself in his
world. "Service" begins: "You can see that nobody lives in / castles like
that / any more / thank God I suppose" (C, 79). This is so flat as to
approximate prose. But if Merwin has made the final adjustment to
natural speech, William Carlos Williams would have approved, for he
believed that "To use even a special posture of speech is to confess an
inability to have penetrated with poetry some crevice of understanding." It is to say "that special things are reserved for art, that it is
unable, that it requires fostering. This is unbearable."[29]

Along with Williams, Merwin admires the poetic faculty of invention. And Merwin would probably endorse Wordsworth's statement in
the Preface to the Second Edition of the *Lyrical Ballads* that spontaneous knowledge of truth "is carried alive into the heart by passion;
truth which is its own testimony, which gives competence and confidence to the tribunal to which it appeals." Poetry is "the spontaneous
overflow of powerful feelings." In the later books of poetry Merwin
writes by a process of what Williams would have called a "seizing on,
the glowing and growing with, what is interesting and nourishing in
the environment."[30]

But Merwin's poetry, as we have already indicated in the preceding
chapter, cannot be measured solely in terms of American and British
literary history. If, as the editors of the *Norton Anthology of Modern
Poetry* say, the "old drunk in the furnace is Orpheus in a new and
wonderful form,"[31] Merwin's thematic disorganization, temporal dis-
locations, and his use of the most startling and unexpected imagery all
draw him closer to the Surrealist tradition in French and Spanish

poetry. He "refines a Surrealist flair for bizarre and sudden transformation of image and perspective and for a continued preoccupation with Death as a kind of manifestation of the absolute. For these reasons he has more frequently been placed with James Wright, Robert Bly, and Pablo Neruda."[32] And, we might add, with André Breton, Yves Bonnefoy, and Pierre Reverdy. But as Carol Kyle points out, "Surrealism in Merwin's poetry is much more than a technique; it is a large, affirmative vision, optimistic in the connections among all things."[33]

Surrealism encourages the wild free play of imagination, but it also tends to limit a writer. Once he begins to write a poetry of extremes, it is difficult to retreat again to a poetry of limits. Irvin Ehrenpreis confronts this problem in a review: "In the poetry of extremes the author usually implies that he does not avoid the rending emotions, that to do so would be hypocritical or cowardly. As an artist he implies that by exposing oneself to such strains, one becomes a true poet. To suffer them unflinchingly is a power that separates insight from bland conventionality. The poet may even sound like a martyr, sacrificing his peace of mind in order to confer on humanity the benefit of his art: Berryman touches this note."[34] But once the poet has given voice to these rending emotions in daring Surrealist progressions, how can he gracefully retire to a more orderly poetry? Could he then treat tragedy, loss, or bereavement while maintaining a cool, ironic distance? Such is not Merwin's ability *or* desire in the late 1970s. Elegant detachment holds no attraction for him. And there are no psychic crises to impel the poetic variety he achieved in earlier books. What remains for him except the adoption of an ordinary language and range of subjects to match the more ordinary character of his present life? The result, a relaxed tone and more prosaic diction, some find disappointing. Merwin no longer sacrifices peace of mind for imaginative truths. Even former enthusiasts are conceding that in the poetry of *The Compass Flower* they find "Something lower." The poems largely sustain a haiku-like objectivity and display bland conventionality. Except for the triumphs of "Kore," the love poems, and "The Vineyard," they stay largely on the literal level and display a monotonous similarity of tone. Merwin no longer communicates directly with other consciousnesses in nature, as he did in *The Carrier of Ladders* where he wrote: "Kestrel and lark shimmer over the high stones / like two brothers who avoid each other / on the cliff corner I met the wind / a brother" (CL, 39). Instead in *The Compass Flower* the regard is distant and detached; he is looking away:

> Sheep and rocks drifting together before sunset
> late birds rowing home across bright spaces
> shadows stroking the long day above the earth
> wild voices high and far-carrying
> at sun's descent toward ripening grain. (C, 46)

Here the stance is passive, retrospective. Poetry is not perceived as an entry into being; the voice is not the strong, active participatory voice of "The Black Plateau." Rather than rendering emotions or sensations directly in *The Compass Flower,* he summons them in memory, and they float across the horizon of the poem. Reality is often seen retrospectively, as through a glass darkly. Even the chronic bitterness which animated *The Lice* and portions of *The Carrier of Ladders* makes no appearance here. The most positive development in this book is that his poetic scope has broadened to include sensuality. He is now writing tender love poetry. "Spring Equinox Full Moon" opens:

> I breathe to you
> love in the south in the many
> months of spring
> hibiscus in dark hair water
> at the source
> shadows glistening to hips
> thighs slender sunset shining shores (C, 59)

For the first time in all his poetry sexuality and the life of the body are fully accepted and celebrated. Now nature is experienced as it enhances the beauty of his beloved; it creates a dynamic environment for their love, while she is the inspired and inspiring center of the poem: "away from you on a corner of the earth / I want to think for six hours of your hair / which is the invention of singing / daughter of islands" (C, 59).

Sadly, some say that the exquisite beauty of six or seven love poems cannot carry the whole book. Some long time admirers and distinguished critics of Merwin's work are remaining silent, and Hayden Carruth asserts in a review that while he "would not link Merwin with the minimalist-conceptualist agitations that seem so conspicuous now in the visual arts, because I think our poets are influenced less by formal considerations than by the substance of other literatures—surrealism, Spanish-American and Oriental writing, etc. . . . [still] the effect is the same, this movement toward expressive but still vague silence,

the written poem that is a guide to an unwritten one."[35] He understands Merwin's newest poetry as an abandonment of the values of language and calls it vague. But perhaps attaining to silence is one of Merwin's goals. It is not a goal that traditionalists would accept as valid: it
is certainly a paradoxical and destructive goal for a poet. Critics who
value skilled use of language and an original style over insights into
transcendence will find Merwin's conscious movement into silence
unattractive and unacceptable. But seen from the point of view of
Writings to an Unfinished Accompaniment, Merwin's seeming
diminishment in *The Compass Flower* may be a sign of increased self-
understanding, a greater ability to love, and an enhanced knowledge
of what concerns him. Still, unfortunately for his audience, as he learns
more and more, he divulges less and less that is concrete. Though his
newest poems lack the imagistic brilliance and variety that characterized his other books, they do radiate a calm self-acceptance, an easy
sensuality, and open-mindedness. There is a sense of being at one with
the universe.

Gary Thompson argues that the recent poetry is written to assist us
in our own growth toward self-understanding and silence, to the end
that "we [might] reach such a strong understanding of ourselves that
we no longer feel the need to speak. We will become silence."[36] This
point is substantiated by Merwin's "On Each Journey":

> As on each journey there is
> a silence that goes with it
> to its end let us go
> with each other
> though the sun with its choirs of distance
> rises between us though it
> were to hang there the past like a day
> that would burn unmoved forever
> and only we went on
> each alone with nothing
> but a silence (W, 20)

"At the Same Time" even indicates that the use of language ultimately
necessitates a movement into silence. It is as if the use of any language
but the primal language is becoming repulsive to him:

> While we talk
> thousands of languages are
> saying nothing

> while we close a door
> flocks of birds are flying through winters
> of endless light
> while we sign our names
> more of us
> lets go
>
> and will never answer (W, 37)

VII   *Ecologist of the Word and World*

In *The Carrier of Ladders* in "Psalm: Our Fathers" Merwin writes:
"I am the son of thanksgiving but its language is strange in my mouth"
(93) and " I am the son of a silence in heaven but I cried and the dark
angels went on falling" (95). If a poem is a cry, Merwin's greatest
desire has been to hear and call out clearly. In "Dogs" in *Writings to
an Unfinished Accompaniment,* a book whose every title suggests the
possibility of a responsive accompaniment, he speaks of the aural
dimensions of loneliness. Initially, he states that loneliness is not being
heard: "Many times loneliness / is someone else / an absence" (81).
Then he advances another premise:

> it is someone else's dog
> that you're keeping
> then when the dog disappears
> . . . it is yourself
> that absence
> but at last it may be
> that you are your own dog
> hungry on the way
> the one sound climbing a mountain
> higher than time (W, 81)

The quixotic progression from an awareness of absence and a yearning
for a person, through the dog's representing that person, to the loss of
the dog, to the transformation of speaker into a dog culminates in a
celebration of the freedom of the open road and wanderlust. "You are
your own dog," just as before he spoke of following the "child that will
lead me." Awareness of self is an awareness—and acceptance—that
the self is "hungry on the way." In "Dogs," the self is happily engaged
in climbing; this motion reverses the usual motion of the stars and

"dark angels," who are "falling," and suggests that the self is eternal. Merwin's description of an individual life as "one sound climbing a mountain" recalls Jean Follain's metaphor for the single human life, "a sound among the sounds of the world / where the bird sang."[37] But Merwin's individual life makes a sound whose pitch grows higher; it ultimately intones a pitch even "higher than time." He indicates that one transcends time in a solitary oneness, in rejoicing in one's own upward movement and the acceptance of responsibility for oneself. Transcendence comes, he implies, when one is out of sight, out of sound. Yet all the while the climbing proceeds, hearing is important.

Having acute hearing is essential to those who want to write in "the great language," "the vernacular of the imagination, which at one time was common to men." This language Merwin defines as a "tongue . . . loosed in the service of immediate recognition, and that in itself would make it foreign in our period. For it conveys something of the unsoundable quality of experience and the hearing of it is a private matter.[38] His use of the word "unsoundable" is curious here. Is he suggesting that few others are or should be capable of mastering this language? It may be that few poets are granted this ability. Emerson observed in "The Poet," "For poetry was all written before time was, and whenever we are so finely organized that we can penetrate into that region where the air is music, we hear those primal warblings and attempt to write them down, but we lose ever and anon a word or a verse and substitute something of our own, and thus miswrite the poem."[39] Just as Merwin is intrigued by the symbolic or "naming" function of language, his definition of "the great language" as a "tongue . . . loosed in the service of immediate recognition" illustrates that he, like Emerson, is an ecologist or preserver of the word as well. Each sought to write in the original language; and because of the rootedness of words in things, each becomes by extension a perserver of all aspects of nature. By attuning his ear and poetic voice to the voice of nature, the poet can perceive nature's language, hear "the original idiom." Enlarging on Emerson's statement that "Every new relation is a new word," Josephine Miles writes, "Names are part of the categorizing force of nature . . . sentences, generalizations, are part of the law of nature . . . [Emerson] accepts image and symbol as vital, from the natural world; and then his contribution as poet is to show them in new relation."[40] "Every new relation is a new word," then the world is "put under the mind for verb and noun" without explicit connective. The poet makes that connective. In his best poetry Merwin finds the vital connectives between natural object and poetic word. Emerson says the poet "re-attaches things to nature and the Whole—re-attaching even artificial things and violation of nature, to nature, by deeper insight."[41]—he is thus an ecologist of the word. Merwin appears to be conscious of the poet's burden of responsibility and of the possibility of his own failure to reattach each word to its proper object. In "Language," a prose poem from *Houses and Travellers,* he reveals the organic connection between human anatomy and certain words: "Certain words now in our knowledge we will not use again, and we will never forget them. We need them. Like the back of the picture. Like our marrow, and the color in our veins. We shine the lantern of our sleep on them, to make sure, and there they are, trembling already for the day of witness. They will be buried with us, and rise with the rest" (H, 58).

Moreover, Merwin is convinced that it is impossible to define man without bringing what he calls "the non-human world" into the definition.[42] In the recent books he does indeed bring "the non-human world" into the poetry: his organization of one book seasonally and his likening himself to aspects of nature reveal an intense rapport with the rhythms, cycles, and spirit of nature. Like the poet of Emerson's essays or the poet of *Song of Myself,* the self in Merwin's best poetry is in intimate contact with the universe, open to inspiration and revelation. One is reminded of Emerson's description of the poet in *Nature:*

The poet, the orator, bred in the woods, whose senses have been nourished by their fair and appeasing changes, year after year, without design and without heed, shall not lose their lesson altogether, in the roar of cities . . . Long hereafter, amidst agitation and terror . . . these solemn images shall reappear in their morning lustre, as fit symbols and words of the thoughts which the passing events shall awaken. At the call of a noble sentiment, again the woods wave, the pines murmur, the river rolls and shines, and the cattle low upon the mountains, . . . And with these forms, the spells of persuasion, the keys of power are put into his hands.[43]

Merwin holds these keys of power and can turn them when he chooses. His best poetry has an informing sense of the unity of the mind with the universe. Beyond this, there is in some of his work a celebration of the visionary dimensions of experience, what Wallace Stevens called, "one's tootings at the weddings of the soul." Merwin has profound knowledge of Emerson's "radical correspondence between visible things and human thought." The self of his most outstanding poems is a self that "touches all edges" of the world in imaginative expansion.

While Emerson's nature could be relied upon to renew herself end-lessly, to "insure herself," as he put it, today reasonable people question her ability to do so. If her ability to manage mankind's technological and nuclear waste is questionable, Merwin relishes the thought that nature might begin to take her own vengeance on man for his ecolog-ical destructiveness. "The Last One" is the world's last tree, the last living part of the "non-human world": "Well they cut everything because why not." Now, in presuming to kill the last one, they are presuming too much. Their hubris is punished by the gods of nature who swallow their shadows and kill them (L, 10–12).

Merwin thinks of nature as a living body. The loss of any part of the body, any species, spells dismemberment or disfiguration. Since the world has undoubtedly lost hundreds, if not thousands, of species of animals that were at the time considered as expendable as the snail darter, part of the "original idiom" has of course vanished forever. Because many words and animals are extinct, the original idiom, like the identity of the poet himself, is flawed and incomplete. All of it can never be recovered: it will remain, as Emerson said, "brute and dark." Merwin writes of "unknown / unknown languages." Every human being alive today, Merwin believes, is subtly affected by this loss. Poets can only attempt to preserve "the loss that has not left this place." Mer-win is only cautiously hopeful in the recent books of poetry while the mood of Emerson's essay is unreservedly hopeful. Merwin's "For a Coming Extinction," published in *The Lice*, paints a grim portrait of the predations of whalers on the gray whale.[44] The poem addresses the gray whale:

> Now that we are sending you to The End
> The great god
> Tell him
> That we who follow you invented forgiveness
> And forgive nothing
> . . . Tell him
> That it is we who are important (L, 68–69)

As parts of the original creation and language move silently into obliv-ion, all life on earth is diminished. And the tone of "For a Coming Extinction" reveals that Merwin is primarily an ethical rather than a political poet. He envisions not the Marxist utopia of the future, but the Biblical utopias—the Eden of the past or Apocalypse of the future. He would, if possible, live with one foot in Eden. But, given even a diminished environment, he will remain conceptually and essentially attached to it. In "Gift" he writes:

> I must be led by what was given to me
> as streams are led to it
> and braiding flights of birds
> the gropings of veins the learning of plants
> the thankful days
> breath by breath (W, 112).

In his greatest writings to an unfinished accompaniment he rediscovers parts of the original idiom, recovering and preserving through translation parts other poets have discovered. For the ecologists and archeologists of the word and world, there exists a community of readers and believers who value their efforts and who also love and understand "the great language."

CHAPTER 6

Parable and Paradox

a strange time
has come upon us like a shadow
Ghalib

W. S. Merwin's prose inhabits a dwelling that seems to disappear, or at least a realm where, as he says in one of his prose poems, "disappearance could be considered a kind of beginning" (MP, 3). Disappearance is the threshold one must cross to penetrate the mysteries of the interior of these prose poems embodying in his negative aesthetic an intimacy of need—"everything that does not need you is real."

I Why Prose?

In *The Miner's Pale Children* (1970) and *Houses and Travelers* (1977) Merwin moves from poetic composition to the more linear associative narrative of the prose poem. He chooses the roughly chronological narrative form characteristic of tales, fables, parables, memories, or fairy tales. Of these prose pieces James Atlas writes:

The Miner's Pale Children exploited a genre that extends from Baudelaire through Rimbaud and Mallarmé to Francis Ponge in France, that shares affinities with Lichtenberg and imitates Kafka: the prose poem. These pieces, less fiction than parable, explore an odd region where events are unexplained, where animals talk among themselves, where hope has been "a calm lake in early spring, white because the sky above it was the color of milk." Like the fables of Donald Barthelme, or Beckett's *stories and texts for nothing*, Merwin's episodic, elusive stories exist in a dimension of the mysterious, spoken through some unidentified voice. The language is dense and detailed, but about nothing, or to be more specific, about the problem of nothingness.[1]

Merwin's prose poem "The Cheese Seller" illustrates this pursuit of the problem of nothingness: "Everything, they say, everything that

129

ever exists even for a moment floats on the black lake, the black lake, and there at each moment what is reflected is its opposite what is reflected is. This is one of the basic truths, without which existence itself would be impossible. How can that be?" (MP, 166) His philosophical reflection on nothingness absorbs the remainder of this roving prose poem. To read it is to join him in a debate, which continues in "Among Mutes": "Even things divulge the form of their desires, if we could read their lips. Everything that is reflected in a window or a polished surface is being judged for its likeness to a glacier. Which may never have existed" (MP, 173). Sometimes playful, sometimes haunting, sometimes wry and witty, the voice of these prose poems meanders on associatively, leaping from figure to figure, conjecture to conjecture; yet surprisingly, the way Merwin's poems and prose poems achieve their impact is nearly the same. Speaking of the progression of one of Merwin's poems, Denis Donoghue describes the progression of both his prose and his poetry: "What is fine in this poem is the tact by which the persuasive implications of the first figure are led, step by step downward, until the meditative pathos [of these implications] is released."[2] Both the prose poem and poem move through a series of figures with persuasive implications. The reader is caught up in exploring these implications for himself until at a final pivotal figure he realizes the pathos latent in the progression. Even the themes treated in *The Miner's Pale Children* and *The Lice* and to some extent *The Carrier of Ladders* are the same: the spectacle is one of loss, fragmentation, forgetting, choice, chance, and departure.

Why prose then? What *is* a prose poem? Michael Benedikt in *The Prose Poem: An International Anthology* defines it as "a genre of poetry, which includes the intense use of devices of verse. The sole exception to access to the possibilities, rather than the set priorities of verse is, we would say, the line break." He signals the word "intense" as especially important in this definition and goes on to stress the fact that the prose poem is more directly and specifically concerned with giving voice to the unconscious. Its movement is dictated by the freer, wider-ranging movement of the unconscious which must not be inhibited by line breaks. "The attention to the unconscious, and to its particular logic, unfettered by the relatively formalistic interruptions of the line break, remains the most immediately apparent property of the prose poem."[3]

The diction and tone of Merwin's prose poems are often subtly dif-

ferent from those of his other poems, however. The language is less
highly charged, emotionally or imagistically. Often the tone of voice
is more matter-of-fact; as is suitable for an extended philosophical discussion or a narrative, the language is more general—some have called
it more vague[4]. Benedikt argues that "The form has often given . . . a
certain tough-mindedness to the representation of the traditionally
'delicate,' tentative realm of inward imagination—an achievement
which is understandably anathema not only to a merely lyrical view of
poetry, but to traditionalist critics attached to it. This new security with
respect to the unconscious has, most strikingly, given rise to writings as
matter-of-fact and direct as that . . . of Kafka, Cortazar, Ponge, and
Merwin. . . ."[5]

Merwin's prose poems, first published in small increments in *The
Moving Target*, explore, like his poetry, the dimensions of mystery and
silence he encounters within. As he writes more and more prose during
the 1960s, he displays a facility and talent for it. Passing beyond his
successful experiments in chant-like orphic poetry in the early 1970s,
he revels in his successful soundings of the collective unconscious in
prose and in the greater freedom of subject matter he permits himself
in it. As Richard Howard notes, his prose shows none of the agony of
the poetry, "no such relentless twist of idiom. For prose is the proper
medium for removals, separations, 'the blandishments of decay,' and
with remarkable ease Merwin parades his mastery of half a dozen
tonalities."[6] This variety of tonalities is far more evident in the first
book of prose than in *Houses and Travellers*, where there is even a
certain uniformity of tone. The styles, too, are more adventurous, var-
ied, and ambitious in the former book than in the latter, where one
style predominates. Each prose poem has a unique focus in *The
Miner's Pale Children*, while in *Houses and Travellers* the pieces are
for the most part narratives; they seem to employ the same three or
four speakers. Each speaker is alone, reflective, yet largely incapable
of understanding the full implications of his plight.

Discussing the contrast between Jean Follain's poems and his prose
poems, Merwin says, "The 'I' is more openly present here than in the
poems . . . it is never confronted but refers—a regard." This distinction
applies to his own work as well. Who is this "I" who says these exact
things or makes these subtle judgments? Merwin provides the answer
to this question in an assessment of Follain's prose poems, which resemble Merwin's in their use of the "I": "The 'I' suspended regard . . . an

'impersonal,' receptive, but essentially unchanging gaze which often occupies, in Follain's work, the place of the first person. . . ."[7] In the prose poems the "I" serves not to reveal character but to conceal it.

II *The Dwelling That Disappears*

The primary emotional impact of the prose poems of *The Miner's Pale Children* is that of fear and danger. All the while, the speaker is powerless to counter the danger or assuage the fear. Consequently, a dim frustration emanates from the first volume of prose: it is more pronounced in his satiric denunciations of the fallen state of contemporary American culture ("Unchopping a Tree" and "Make this Simple Test") and less pronounced in the philosophical speculations ("Blue" and "Songs of the Icebergs"). But the undertone of loss and frustrated hope reflects all the aridity in America's dominant religion, materialism. All the fear and anger awakened in liberals by the VietNam war lurks here in frozen hysteria. In an interview Merwin conjectured, "if the feeling of crisis goes on long enough . . . one of two things happens—either a person or a society becomes numbed or they get involved in poetry."[8]

America for Merwin in the early 1970s acutely presented the problem of nothingness. A contemporary prose poem titled "The Dwelling" reveals his own personal fear of loss of being:

Once when I looked at myself there was nothing. I could not see any size, any shape, any color. I could tell that I was still there because I was frightened, and I could feel that. When I began to think about myself it kept coming down to that, as though that was the only thing to remember. Yes, that was the only thing I could remember about myself clearly and accurately. I was frightened. The one thing went back until I vanished with it. The point of that disappearance could be considered a kind of beginning. And now to the original dread this new fear was added: that I might forget that I was afraid, and so vanish again, entirely.
The new fear was a revelation. (MP, 3)

Jan B. Gordon comments on this, "The opening parable of W. S. Merwin's prose volume, *The Miner's Pale Children*, is in effect a discourse upon the nature of being. . . . Only the fear of the absence of substance gives evidence of presence, so that terror is a kind of first condition of creation. But this very terror is a thing of permanence thanks to a philosophical and psychological multiplier-effect: one lives in terror that he might forget the terror of his first vanishing."[9] Merwin says, in effect, "I fear I shall vanish, therefore I am." Although the fear expressed in the prose poem is easily recognizable, his final revelation is perplexing. This revelation provides him with the possibility of a comfortable entry into non-being and hence in the prose there ensues a "moment of precarious rejoicing." The entire prose poem in fact traces an entry into non-being: "oblivion never left my side." The poet and oblivion converse together: you might say they become fast friends. In the remaining lines of "The Dwelling," the speaker builds a dwelling for his primal fear, giving it a local habitation and preserving *it*, at least, from oblivion.

In "Being Born Again" (MP, 46–48) Merwin conceives of the self as existing in "many forms at a given time . . . one of which I think I am used to and have adopted as a convention." If the selves we are conscious of are conventional roles assumed so as to carry on normally in society, the possibility exists that a new self might come to birth, much as Gregor the salesman brought to birth Gregor the enormous insect in Kafka's "The Metamorphosis." In Merwin's prose poem the travail of labor pains is physically experienced as the poem treats the experience of bringing to birth one of the unconscious selves that populate the speaker's identity:

> However I move or wherever I go I cannot get outside of this travail, which in itself, of course, is a delivery from a confinement. The heaven and earth of this predicament are nowhere that I can see. . . . And the pressure has come from some other existence of myself, unknown to me or at least unnoticed, that has grown, curled in itself, until it can no longer be contained and is now undergoing a change in its very cosmos. (MP. 46)

The senses cannot experience or appropriate the new self: "My senses cannot place that other being, nor define it. They can only learn of it by leaving it. Then the suffering will remain with them. Like a root torn out. It will have become the first possession, the first knowledge of the new 'I.'" Just like the old "I," the new "I" will exist in suffering and be experienced in suffering. To have an independent identity as a self is tantamount to experiencing suffering. He pursues this point in "The Sentinel": "They believe that each child is invested at birth with its particular grief which will never willingly forsake it afterwards" (MP, 93–95). One cannot tell who "they" are from the context, but the fact remains that each child's particular grief is its sentinel watching over it like a guardian angel. The watching grief is

"Something more personal than a name, something in fact for which the name is a blank symbol. Something never seen by its host or by others, yet with features, a voice, a touch, that no one could mistake, even in disguise. Something that will be inseparable, for as long as he lives, from whatever each person calls 'me.'" Kafka was convinced that one cannot live without a belief in something indestructible in oneself, yet this indestructible element constantly eludes one. Merwin's indestructible, inseparable grief may be exactly the element Kafka envisioned. A knowledge of a native grief might have attracted Kafka whose doorkeeper sermon can be summed up, "There is infinite hope, but not for us."

"The Sentinel" continues: "It was his grief that promised to complete him, and continually renews the promise." Merwin gives a negative definition of man—a definition of what he is *not*—in a description of a creature of an earlier era who was born without grief: "He was not curious. He had not conceived of heaven. He did not dream. He was not complete. Only in this last detail was he already man." The implications of this reverse definition are that one can only know oneself through a slow process of understanding what one is not.

Of primary interest to Merwin is "unnameable stillness that unites" (MP, 56) all the senses. This stillness lies "at the heart of change . . . unseeing, unhearing, unfeeling, unchanging" and is essentially inaccessible by way of the senses. Stillness is the voice of the self coming to us: "We are the voice . . . That is what we are doing here. It has to pass through us. It has to pass through us in order to reach us. It has to go through us without pausing in order to be clear of us. . . . The stillness is not in the senses but through them and the voices must come through the stillness . . . we must become transparent" (MP, 57). In the stillness one apprehends the essential self, "the voices must come through the stillness." The voices in their calling never change, but each individual changes in every way as he progresses through life. What puzzles Merwin is, "Will we be able to receive it?" Hearing the voices and responding to them constitutes life's mission; it is hearing the silence in the human soul, hearing the soul in silence. The mystery of being can only be framed in paradox.

He presents a clearer if no less ambiguous definition of the self in "The Abyss": "On occasions . . . I open my eyes, and instead of the world where the days have names and belong to weeks, I see that I am really still hanging by my breath, high in space, with night already advanced and no prospect of a morning . . . I dare not call. Who would

I call? Silently, watching the shadowy valley rise and sink below me,
I say to my breath once again, little breath come from in front of me,
go away behind me, row me quietly now, as far as you can, for I am
an abyss that I am trying to cross" (MP, 183–4). A person gains a sense
of self, then, only derivatively. He has to wait for spontaneous knowledge of the abyss within. Merwin's "What We Are Named For"
explains this:

> To say what or where we came from has nothing to do with what or where
> we came from. We do not come from there any more, but only from each
> word that proceeds out of the mouth of the unnamed.
> And yet sometimes it is our only way of pointing to who we are. (MP, 132)

We are not named for objects or persons in a "world where the days
have names and belong to weeks." Each of us is "really still hanging"
by his breath and is named for "each word that proceeds out of the
mouth of the unnamed."

As Jan Gordon explains, "Poetic language is language thrown out
indeterminately at an object, but historical language grants us the
determinacy of the proper name."[10] Gordon clarifies the polarity
between poetic and historical language, poetry and history, in Merwin's work, with reference to the epigraph of *The Lice*—"What we
have caught and . . . killed we have left behind, but what has escaped
us we bring with us":

> The equation of death and history is a *donnée* of Merwin's universe, for
> history is precisely that aspect of the "hidden" which man has caught and
> killed. Fantasy, its opposite, is that aspect of our past which has escaped the
> murderous trivialization of associative succession. Fantasy creates an implicit
> equation between distance and desire which creates barriers and boundaries
> in turn. The distinction between history and fantasy is, in effect, a distinction
> between that aspect of our collective past which we have appropriated (his-
> tory, death, guilt) and that which remains inscrutable save as an object
> against which language might be directed.[11]

If history is the form of grief or "despair reserved for the living," it is
also what has failed to become of us. One mask of Janus, the liminary
deity, looks backward onto the past—that is history—but another looks
forward. This mask is the "other half of grief"; it gazes into a realm of
fantasy and poetry where everything has its designation though it may
not be namable since the words may no longer fit their intended

objects. Merwin realizes that it is harder to look forward than to look
back. There is a comforting definiteness about the past which is allur-
ing: "When you look back there is always the past / Even when it has
vanished" (L, 17). But to look forward is to look into nothingness, hence
his negative aesthetic. Poetry exists in this realm of comparative inde-
terminacy; entering this realm affords the poet a means of escaping the
living death of history. The epigraph of *The Lice* directly refers to the
relationship between "temporal values and what we might call 'the
hidden' . . . History is precisely that aspect of 'the hidden' which man
has caught and killed; it is the record of the de-naturalization of nature.
Through her prescriptions, we attempt to give internalized rhythms an
external referent."[12] Poetry allows internalized rhythms and language
to remain intimate, subjective, and personal. It refuses to kill them
through imposition of an arbitrary determinacy, a killing order. "The
Hydra" is written about the monster of history; it contrasts poets who
study the living language of the grass with the purposeful but dying
historians:

> I was young and the dead were in other
> Ages
> As the grass had its own language . . .
>
> One thing about the living sometimes a piece of us
> Can stop dying for a moment
> But you are dead
>
> Once you go into those names you go on you never
> Hesitate
> You go on (L, 5).

History fixes the names, quantifies, weighs, and numbers human events
and human beings so that there is no way the past can stop dying once
it has gone "into those names." Poets live and write in a world apart
from the falling-into-named-oblivion which is history. Poets listen to
the language of the grass and of nature. Or they climb Hunger Mountain to see the "view of the Promised Land. Most who have come to
tell went only part way . . . even they have seen things that no one else
ever saw, things they could not describe, too hard for the words, and
then too hard for them, the witnesses. But certain ones who never forgot and who never sleep gave us their words to eat. They buried their
words in us and went away, leaving us hungry, part way" (H,104). In
"Hunger Mountain" from *Houses and Travellers* he speaks of the rov-

ing poets who bring back their visions which are "too hard for the words" and too hard for the witnesses. But they nourish the people on what words they can summon to apply to the experience, giving "us their words to eat." Their burial of the words keeps the precious treasure of revelations safe from marauders or scoffers and, more important, it keeps it from entering history.

The vision of poetry condemned to enter history motivates Merwin to write "Ship":

> Far from here but still in sight
>
> there is a fine white ship of everything we have loved
> under full sail entering
> among wrecks and many bridges
> where birds are watching
> always watching
> same birds
> with one wing
>
> forgetters of singing
>
> here it is they see coming to them again
> for those who hate them (W, 60)

The debacles and transitory periods of history are "wrecks and many bridges." Historians, "forgetters of singing," are "always watching." They are the birds "with one wing," so naturally they do not fly. In the final stanza we enter their consciousness briefly: "here it is," they think. The last line reveals the hatred the poets on "a fine white ship of everything we have loved" bear for their watchers. Anyone who would presume to account for, measure, or analyze the poets' treasures could be grouped with the "forgetters of singing" since he is more absorbed in "always watching" than in fulfilling his own creativity. When this author first contacted Merwin to inform him she had launched a full-scale treatment of his work, he sent her "Ship." One might infer from this that he thinks of critics and students of poetry, this author among them, as the "same birds." He habitually ignores critics and does not especially like the idea of having his poetry scrutinized. Once it is written and published, he gradually moves away from it until it is consigned to history. Who knows whether or not he savors the ultimate irony of this?

"Ship" implies that the fine white ship is sailing toward shipwreck.

It proudly challenges those who hate it, persisting in sailing right into their midst. Extinction is a central horror in Merwin's poetry, and it makes its reappearance here and in many prose poems, particularly in "The Dwelling" where the speaker's native fear is a fear of vanishing. Gordon explains, "Extinction, like the terror of vanishing of which Merwin spoke in 'The Dwelling' is, on one level, the moment at which nature becomes art, and on another, the emergence of historical awareness."[13] Immortalized in a fossil, the living being assumes the fixed form of an art work, a form whose very presence stimulates historical awareness.

III   *Memory, A Blindfolded Deity*

Merwin distrusts the memory: he considers it the deity of historians. All the prose poems seriously question the supposed benefits of having a scrupulously clear memory. "Memory," for example, asks, "In the first place is it a virtue after all? We despise those who are deficient in it, but that may be nothing but our predilection for those deceits that have hoodwinked us in particular . . . like the rest of the blindfolded deities, it is a source of terrible arrogance. It persuades us that nothing of the past remains except what we remember. From there it is only a step to persuading us that the present too would be meaningless without it" (MP, 28–9). *That* is the error in investing in memory.

Commonly, people pride themselves on having sharp memories. To them memory is a virtue, like superior judgment or a love of justice. Justice, by the way, is another of "the blindfolded deities" Merwin refers to here. But, he argues, to trust in one's own memory exclusively and to consider it wholly reliable is "a source of terrible arrogance." It is to act as though "nothing of the past remains except what we remember." This in fact is the theme of "The Remembering Machines of Tomorrow," a brazen satire on those who consign their entire memories to computers. Each computer-owner feeds into the machine not just the whole of his past but "the whole of his present—or of what he takes to be the present. The neat almost soundless instrument will contain all of each man's hope, his innocence, his garden. Then one by one, but with growing frequency, men will begin to lose their machines" (MP, 131).

Obviously to dwell too steadily on memory, coloring the whole of one's present with it is to eclipse the present, losing it to past association. In "Memory" Merwin illustrates how this occurs when Odysseus returns to Ithaca after twenty years' absence. Upon his arrival he tells himself he is pacing "the familiar shore" when in fact he does not remember Ithaca at all: the real Ithaca and his personal sense of his own presence in the place have long since been obliterated by the long voyage. Odysseus's unwittingly hypocritical pride exemplifies the terrible arrogance Merwin abhors. The author has his revenge in portraying Odysseus as a fool and in recording that Odysseus remarked "the same unimpressed absence on the hills." Just as he remembers nothing and no one, so the hills reflect absence and are as unimpressed as ever by him. "If he thought he detected a slight echo to his voice in the first moments it was gone by the time he listened for it. Even the unpleasant details—the screaming of one of the local hysterics, the smell of the back premises of the port, the crabbed features of a neighbor, the resumption of insoluble disputes and onerus responsibilities, were exactly as he had remembered them. He told himself that he had sweetened nothing, that he had been just" (MP, 29). This is Merwin at his most searingly ironic. Surely Merwin has greater compassion for the local hysterics than he does for Odysseus or than Odysseus has for anyone he will encounter in Ithaca. He portrays Odysseus as a well-oiled machine who goes through his paces deliberately, justly, responsibly. Apparently the returning hero is altogether dead—a dead person singular.

This hero, "convinced that his guide through all the weavings has been . . . wisdom itself," is hermetically sealed off from the vulnerability of new meetings or the possibility of fresh insights into Ithaca due to his imperturbable confidence. But Merwin has no faith in the ability of guides to prepare anyone to face the present on his own. Contact with the present both motivates and provides a subject for all his poems in prose and verse. And contact "cannot be routine, stereotyped, or merely conservative because it must cope with the novel, for only the novel is nourishing." Behind all Merwin's writing is what William Carlos Williams calls "invention" or "spontaneity." Similarly, writing *and* true knowledge of self come, as Williams said, from "seizing on, and glowing and growing with, what is interesting and nourishing in the environment."[14] New self-knowledge may be the reward for patience and fortitude; more often it comes to the hungry, those who have been left part way to illumination and are conscious of this. Only their creative work enables them to "hold in one mind reality and justice." Only the knowledge that makes its appearance unannounced, unheralded, and unexpected is the knowledge that rightfully belongs to the individual. It is all he can call his. Anything else Merwin considers a "bought dream." And he asks, "What can you learn from a bought dream?" (H, 66)

Odysseus is unprepared for the flash of spontaneous, intuitive memory he experiences on his third day in Ithaca. The prose poem enters his stream of consciousness in the final paragraph, registering his amazement: "Then why, by the third day—the day of resurrections— this bewilderment, this sense of being utterly lost, of turning, without a goal, in a great emptiness that, for all he knew, reached to the end of the world? Here was something he had not remembered. Something that he never seemed to be able to remember. That same oppression that he had endured so often in this very place, that he had left with anguish and relief and now recognized with a stunned dread. What could he call it? His own presence in the place? The standing on the needle? The present?" (MP, 29)

Only on the third day, "the day of resurrections," does his memory spontaneously reevoke the place and his agonized sense of himself in this place. His calm, purposeful rationality is overwhelmed by his visceral reaction to the place; he becomes aware of this horror of "his own presence in the place, the standing on the needle," the contact with the present moment. He has been out of touch with himself, and hence with his intuitional memory—hence his surprise and "sense . . . of turning, without a goal" in an abyss. When at last he recognizes Ithaca, his old sense of his own presence in the place returns. Appropriately, this self-realization and influx of self-knowledge comes on the third day, the day traditionally set for resurrections. He is now a live person singular: Odysseus is resurrected.

The traditional Western view of knowledge is materialistic and causal: Westerners tend to learn through following instructions and attending to instructors. To the extent that knowledge, for Merwin in his later poems, is not a matter of following instructions but of loving something enough to intuit how it works, his view of knowledge is Eastern. Learning and memory are, for him, uncaused and nonsequential processes. What is known is not acquired systematically, it cannot be drilled into one; instead one learns in intuitive breakthroughs like that Odysseus experienced. What is a logical impossibility in the West—that knowledge should come freely and spontaneously—is a working premise for Merwin. He writes of "the 'freedom' that accompanies poetry at a distance and occasionally joins it, often without being recognized, as in some proverbs. ('God comes to see without a bell,' 'He that lives on hope dances without music') (O, 279).

Whole cultures and religions are based on this idea of knowledge. If it seems strange to the Western mind, that is because Merwin has the temperament of the East.

IV   *Fragments*

Spontaneous self-knowledge or knowledge of the outside world is an individual's one true possession. This knowledge inheres in "each word that proceeds out of the mouth of the unnamed" (MP, 132). "Fragments" (MP, 231–3) speaks of a similar kind of possession that could contain "all of each man's hope, his innocence, his garden." In this prose poem part of a human body appears and disappears for a speaker who keeps a lonely vigil in a blank landscape. It is difficult to know how to take this poem: it could be a satire, but it could also be understood as the account of a humbler Odysseus's awakening. He starts, "I am beginning at last to have moments when something tells me of the miracle. I can be no more specific than that. Not yet."

The scene of his first "intimation" (of immortality?) is "the high room" or upper room where he finds "the hand. All by itself. Palm up. Clean. Empty." In a reversal of the usual divine revelation he encounters not the holy one himself but his relic. This first fragment, the hand palm up, obsesses him and ushers in a period of religious turmoil: "What was it for? Yes, I realized after a time that this was the question I had been asking since the beginning. No, not asking: embodying." The comedy derives from the fact that the speaker is not primarily concerned with the symbolic portent of this discovery but with the loss of the hand to its owner. The speaker chastises himself, in a parody of the self-abasement of Kafka's heroes, for his "self-centered way" and his incomprehension of the historical destiny of the hand. "Now it seemed to me that I was standing as a single spot in a progression too vast for me to even imagine more than a section of it, the progression which represented the story of the hand." Merwin parodies not religion but religious self-abasement which can diminish the worth of the individual. And the phrase "standing as a single spot" recalls Odysseus's intense awareness of standing in the present as a fearful "standing on the needle." In each instance to stand rooted in a single spot or pinned on the needle is to resist involvement or participation in what Words-

worth called "this *living* universe." It is to disallow one's own heritage
and responsibility—movement into the flow and flux of life. It is to
resist life and hence one's own humanity and engagement in all of life.
From stasis no vital knowledge or work can come, hence both speakers
have looked back and been turned into pillars of salt like Lot's wife.

But having plumbed these depths in "Fragments," Merwin proceeds
to effect another third-day resurrection of its speaker. He discovers
"the ear—what was it on its way to hear? Then the ankle, the hair, the
tongue. What am I but a caravanserai whose very walls belong to the
cameldrivers?" The tone subtly mocks the humbleness of the speaker.
He may even sense, as the speaker does in "The Smell of Cold Soup"
(MP, 164), that all these fragments are "leaking from some other part
of your life to which your eyes, and indeed all your other senses, are
closed. Is it from some sector or plane that you have forgotten? Is it, in
that case, from somewhere you have been?"

Toward the end of "Fragments," as in "Memory," the voice changes
and Merwin plunges into the stream of consciousness of the finder of
fragments:

> Five thousand had come to hear him, and some had travelled a long way
> and were hungry. What was there for them to hear? One of those who were
> with him said, "There is a boy here with five loaves and two little fish, but
> what are they among so many?" But he said, "Let them be given to everyone
> who is hungry." And when everyone had eaten his fill the fragments were
> gathered up and they filled twelve baskets.
>
> I mention this because when I found the tongue it came to me for the first
> time that the miracle was not the matter of quantity but the fact that the
> event had never left the present. Parts of it keep appearing. I have begun to
> have glimpses of what I am doing, crossing the place where they have all
> been satisfied, and still finding fragment after fragment.

The first paragraph above is paraphrased from the biblical accounts
of the feeding of the five thousand. Instead of poetry attempting to
transcend or extricate itself from history, as is usual in Merwin, here
an aspect of biblical history is integrated into the prose poem. Though
the lyric could not accommodate such material, the prose poem does.
And it also encompasses parodies like the parody of Kafka's parables
and literary borrowings like this borrowing from the Bible, which itself
reconciles poetry and history.

The final paragraph returns the reader to the speaker's stream of
consciousness. His words have an earnestness and a visionary dimen-

sion no longer undercut by an authorial irony. The revelation involves the poet's reattaching fragments of the original whole: through this reattaching comes a dawning self-knowledge and knowledge of the miracle. The word "fragments," used toward the end of each rhythmical paragraph accrues a symbolic meaning as it comes to mean not simply severed fragments but the numinous ones he occupies himself with collecting: he reassembles the sacred body, the corpus of the transcendent.

Loss is understood by Merwin as one *donnée* of the human condition. He writes, "The voice must have come. Because it is gone" (MP, 58). And in an important prose poem "Speech of a Guide" (H, 60–70) we learn "The things that you lost by the way were guiding you. And you tried to replace them." Any material loss is compensated for by a spiritual gain and any spiritual gain entails a material loss. If the self is divided and knows itself in departure, then any substantial gain must be achieved through experiencing loss. The poet Rainer Maria Rilke asserted much the same thing when he said, "Every single angel is terrible!"[15] Yet every single angel for Rilke—or loss for Merwin—is a guide to the other realm that is "what we are named for." "And it was still guiding you," Merwin cautions, "still crying 'Repent,' from a wild place. But you did not know how to follow it any better than before. You did not attend to the fact that it knew its way in and out of your life better than you did, even knowing where to wait for you, which you would not have known." Your guide, or grief, has been waiting for you like an angel, yet your life has constantly disavowed its existence and disregarded its designs. "So you went on losing and losing, as the rain loses, the mountain loses, the sun loses, as everything under heaven loses. You came along together and here you are." The paradox of being alone yet accompanied by unacknowledged accompaniment is signalled in the oxymoron "alone together." And here human loss is conceived as a natural and vital aspect of a fulfilled destiny: it is integral with the natural losses of rain, mountain, sun, and "everything under heaven." Finally "you" come "alone together" to the implied revelation that to live is to lose because to lose forces resignation, a scaling down of expectations. This lowliness of spirit enables one to journey "under heaven" without bumping one's pride.

The "here you are" of the ending of "Speech of a Guide" carries us back to "the place where they have all been satisfied" in (and by) "The Fragments." Those who were filled with wisdom there or on Hunger Mountain write a poetry which itself crosses and recrosses this place of union and reunion, reassembling the body of the original language, finding the fragments of names. Even history's determinism might be forced back upon itself by those who truly live in and experience the present and who attend to their guides. History's forcing of names and creatures into extinction can be reversed. Mere awareness of the present is one treasure that is each individual's valid possession. "Treasure" envisions the diggers for the words buried earlier on Hunger Mountain; the diggers realize that all their knowledge of history is useless in this endeavor:

> As we begin to dig we find that we are not the first. For all our knowledge of history, we are surprised. Others have dug before us. Did they find it? Did they take it away? How did they hear it was there? Was it there? Was it ever there? Why? What was it, really? Is it still there? What happened to them?
> And that, again, is history. Which leaves us in ignorance.
> We continue to dig. No one has been before us tomorrow.
> And we dig alone. The true present is a place where only one can stand, who is standing there for the first time. (H, 159)

The poet stands in the present each day for the first time. He digs alone, an archaeologist pursuing the secrets of the past which are prophetic of his own future. In "The Track" the poet sees an extinct ancestor's paw track that changes his understanding of himself:

> To see that an ancestor has reappeared
> as the print of a paw
> in a worn brick
> changes what you believe you are
> and where you imagine you are going
> before the clay sets
>
> and what you think might follow you . . .
>
> and when (W, 109)

Seeing the non-human ancestor's paw print precipitates a recognition of their common original nature and of the bond tying the human to the non-human aspects of creation. He realizes his communality with the other animals, some of whom may actually share a vocal language, not simply a physical language of signs and sounds. The print might then be considered the extinct ancestor's word, its message to those who might read it. The print changes—as Charles Darwin's findings change—one's basic understanding of his own existence, of the meaning of being human and whole, not fragmented in a fragmenting world. It alters, ever so subtly, "where you imagine you are going / before the clay sets" and your print is impressed for all eternity.

To look too intently into the Medusa face of history renders one personally helpless, incapable of digging for the treasures the present can offer. Only in imaginative expansion can one rediscover and reattach the fragments of the world's primal unity. The fragments' reappearance seems foreordained, an element in "a progression too vast for me to even imagine more than a section of . . . a progression which represented the story . . . the destiny. . . . " In a concurrent poem, "Midnight in Early Spring," he conceives of these signs as "some alien blessing . . . / granted to the prayerless / in this place." And he inquires:

> who were you
> cold voice born in captivity
> rising
> last martyr of a hope
> last word of a language
> last son
> other half of grief
> who were you (CL, 75)

The speaker's questions find no answer here. These emanations are not willed, as Merwin wrote to Paul Carroll, but emerge as spontaneous as flashes of insight. The possibility of union exists in aesthetic expression at its freest and most expansive or in imaginative receptivity to the transcendent.

If division and absence dwell within the disappearing self, fragments of the early miracles do recur inexplicably, not coincidentally, to the one who is awake to "the true present." Part of the whole body of man, of the "last son" can be recollected wondrously even if one's own past cannot be. If in "The Fragments" the alert watcher in the high room finds what he considers to be part of the body of the Messiah, there is some hope that extinct species and words and whole languages may ultimately be found. In "Language" (H, 58) Merwin discusses "certain words" which we need "Like our marrow, and the color in our veins . . . there they are, trembling already for the day of witness. They will be buried with us, and rise with the rest." They emerge spontaneously in dreams when "we shine the lantern of our sleep on them, to make sure." Here they are believed to be waiting to be "buried with us" so as to "rise with the rest"—on the day of the Second Coming? They and every other life will be judged on "the day of witness."

"He Who Makes Houses" (H, 42–43) is he who is a poet: the poet constructs word-houses. In *Houses and Travellers* (Houses *for* Travellers?) Merwin declares that the house of the poem, especially a prose poem, can be a wildlife refuge for words or a secure retreat for the traveller who comes along to the present alone. This archetypal traveller/poet is pictured in "He Who Makes Houses," a life study of an ideal poet. In this prose poem, Merwin tells of a man, a fablemaker by profession, who makes all kinds of houses. This poem embodies or houses Merwin's own dream of himself at work:

He had lived simply. He looked like wax, but somewhere he was burning. He was always bent at his labor, even when he seemed to be looking at you. His eyes were always on his love, which was the work of his life. He made tools, habits, passages, hiding places, traps, cupboards, pictures, furry corridors, ice chimneys, rotted stairs, laid tables, smells, and bone-filled dens, of lives. Out of everything he could find, beg, borrow, or take away until he could try it first, he made these houses, of all sizes, opening onto every prospect, or dug into the ground. Everywhere that he could persuade someone to let him use the space and let him alone there for a while, he made those houses. He made them on some of the oldest, and on some of the poorest places, and on many others.

Although this account could rightfully apply to Merwin's work in verse as well, it seems a more appropriate description of his work in prose. The variety of subject matter in the prose poems makes them as eclectic as the builder in this poem. They share a wider variety of speakers and tones. Some readers feel at home in the rangier, looser, sometimes baggier prose poems. A weary traveller finds a snug corner there and can put up his feet without harming the furniture. In the poems in verse there is always the possibility that a delicately crafted verse form or a subtle line may be marred by any intrusion; but the prose is eclectic, hewn out of all available scraps: "out of everything he could find, beg, borrow, or take away until he could try it first, he made these houses, of all sizes, opening onto every prospect, or dug into the ground." Other presences, even literary echoings, only enhance the prose poems.

Merwin's first prose poems were the "miner's pale children," treasured products of his conscientious digging. And the poems in that first volume of prose range in length from a few lines to fifteen pages. They have skylights or balconies opening onto every prospect. Their function is to startle one into reflection. The reader travels through Merwin's book, finding other houses, inhabiting each for a while, and then perhaps journeying on to build his own. It does appear that Merwin's chief critics, in fact nearly all his critics, are poets themselves.

Since he makes residences on earth for words, he who builds houses knows the essential nature of words:

> At least once a year—he would explain, when you could get him to answer you—all the words fly up from the places where they have been discontented. For a moment so small that you do not notice it, they leave their comfortless and insecure lodgings altogether, and fly through the air like a swarm of bees. Some people can hear them. He, for instance, could hear them. During those moments which even to him seemed indescribably short, the words manage to travel great distances. Each time it happens that some of them never get back, or end up in other places and nobody knows it, and after that, more people do not understand something, many things, each other, themselves, or all of these. (H, 42–3)

He who makes houses is alert to words becoming detached from their meanings and thus he is better able to build them lodgings that are suited for them, not "comfortless and insecure." He is aware of a general breakdown in communication occurring throughout the community because people "do not understand" that "they are not even using words that live in the same places any more" (H, 43).

Having made a study of words and of their craft, the poet sees that "if each of the words had the house that was right for it, it would go on living there, or if it did go away for a while it would want to come back to the same place." Apparently, having constructed a sound house for words, a living poem where they can reside contentedly, he can watch them return to it like swallows returning every spring. For a poet to find that house takes work, skill, foresight, acute knowledge of the way of words. To build the right houses makes one's reputation as a poet. James Atlas observes, "Ponge, during a conversation with Philippe Sollers, described his own writings, or texts, as materialistic, in that words become 'une réalité concréte, comportant toute l'évidence et l'épaisseur des choses du monde extérieur.' [a concrete reality, bearing the evidence and thickness of the things of the external world]." Atlas indicates that this is what Merwin has achieved in these prose pieces, the lesson of which could be: "to write is to determine the world's actual properties."[16] In the relaxed gait but intense gaze of the prose poem, Merwin spins his quirky, rambling tales, reminiscent of Kafka's parables or Borges's labyrinths in narrative, because, as he says in "Nothing Began As It Is," "Everything has its story" (H, 5).

V Paradox: You Are the Second Person

In 1971, the year after *The Miner's Pale Children* was published, Merwin was awarded the Pulitzer Prize for *The Carrier of Ladders*. While accepting the prize itself, he chose to give away the prize money because "after the years of the news from Southeast Asia and the commentary from Washington, I am too conscious of being an American," to accept it. To Merwin's chagrin, America exerts her primacy over the other nations of the world: she insists she is "the first person." His poetry and prose, however, register a phenomenology of ruin. He observes that everything America's imperialistic materialism touches turns to gold. She, like Midas, cannot nourish herself spiritually because of her golden touch, nor can she hear those like Merwin who speak to her of what concerns her. "I am too conscious of being an American," he observed, "to accept public congratulation with good grace, or to welcome it as an occasion for expressing openly a shame which many Americans feel, day after day, helplessly and in silence."[17] He considers Americans some of the most destructive and rapaciously greedy of the world's human beings.

Merwin's prose poem "The Second Person" (MP, 116–7) cleverly marshalls grammatical evidence to substantiate a political and ethical point. He opens in preemptory tones. Conceivably, he is addressing America: "You are the second person." Historically Americans have assumed they are the first persons, ignorant of the fact that highly developed civilization had existed for thousands of years prior to their arrival on this continent.

In the second paragraph of the poem, the gaze shifts to "you" and your discomfort. Like Eliot's J. Alfred Prufrock, the "you" under scrutiny experiences embarrassment at being "formulated, sprawling on a pin": "You look around for someone else to be the second person. But there is no one else. Even if there were someone else there they could not be you. You try to shelter in imagining that you are plural." But your guilt is personal, singular, and unavoidable. He pricks the bubble of national ego, challenging Yankee pride in individualism.

"No, you insist, it is all a mistake, I am the first person." "But," he enjoins, "you know how unsatisfactory that is. And how seldom it is true." Since "you" are "made in the image of The Second Person, you never see your face"; therefore how seldom it is true that "you" are or should be the first person. Satirizing American trumpeting of "our country right or wrong " he shows how seldom it is true that Americans are the first persons in any of the senses that the phrase will bear.

Through his translations Merwin tries out other voices and other ways of knowing and thinking poetically; he avoids American First Personhood or American cultural chauvinism. His extensive and intensive work in translation enables him to try out other modes of poetry. Through experiencing what it is to think and create in other minds, he experiences other worlds of consciousness, some more sacred and erotic than his own—in the translation of *Sanskrit Love Poetry* (1977), for example—and some more satiric, trenchant, and earthy than his own—in his translations of Chamfort (1969). No American Plato is needed to expel this poet from his Republic, for Merwin seeks an international citizenship in another republic, a republic of poetry. He wants to establish, through his work of saving poetry through translation, a camaraderie of equals in the world of poetry.

Merwin uses translation as a means of effacing the primacy of the Western ego, a primacy inbred in him and all other Americans. Though, technically speaking, his translations are not within his own poetic corpus, still they reflect and even extend his imaginative range and sensibility. In translating, the author is always "the second person": he is not the author but the translator. He is only first in his capacity as a disseminator of poetry that might otherwise go unread in this country. In fact, when the literary histories of the late twentieth century are written, Merwin may well be remembered and honored as much for his copious translations of ancient, anonymous, and lesser known poetry as for his own poetry. With the possible exception of his translation of the Angolan Agnostinho Neto, Merwin never translates a poet for political motives. Nor is he motivated by an urge to enhance his own prestige: he would not translate Rilke merely because Rilke is in vogue. His translations make available to his American and British readers poetry that they might otherwise miss. He merely finds an obscure poet *he* likes and shares his work with all the readers of his translations.

Although his *Selected Translations 1948-1968* (published in 1969) contains Catullus and the *then* lesser known Russian poets Jacob Brodsky and Osip Mandelstam, one quarter of the book is devoted to early anonymous poetry from such disparate countries as Spain, Egypt, Wales, Kabylia, and Greece. Among the French poets he presents here are Jean Follain, Henri Michaux, and LeConte Delisle, none of whom had been widely read in this country before 1969. There is also a good selection of medieval Spanish ballads, many of them anonymous, and French Renaissance and neoclassical poetry. Of the poetry by known poets, several of the authors come from nations not universally recognized for their excellent poetry—nations like Angola and VietNam. Because of the lyrical purity and variety and intrinsic merit of these selections, reading this book of translations from all over the world would afford the beginning reader of poetry a fine introduction to the genre; Philip Levine has suggested precisely this.[18]

VI   *The Translations*

Merwin's translation is motivated by zeal and love for particular poems. In his translation as a whole he has concentrated on a wide variety of literate and brilliant writers, ancient and modern. He is one of the most highly educated, ingenious translators working in America today, and his list of translations ranges from the satires of Persius to the maxims of Chamfort, from *The Cid* and *The Song of Roland* to the aphorisms of Antonio Porchia, from *Lazarillo de Tormes* and *Some Spanish Ballads* to a collection of poems by Osip Mandelstam. In the 1950s and 1960s, Merwin translated Pablo Neruda, Juan Ramón Jiménez, and Federico García Lorca, but more recently he has chosen to bring out a book of poetry by Roberto Juarroz. He follows the same pattern of moving from the known to unknown poets in French poetry. Of the modern poets, first he translated René Char and Yves Bonnefoy; but in 1969 he published an entire book of poetry by Jean Follain, then virtually unknown in the United States. His inclination of late has been to resurrect and make available to the reading public more and more obscure poets and poetry; but as in the past, whoever Merwin introduces is immediately read and brought into the literary mainstream. In another decade these lesser known poets and their works will be part of the cultural currency and standard reading for lovers of poetry.

As the body of translations is too large to discuss in any but cursory fashion, a few examples of Merwin's translations and some brief notes on his method must suffice. In the Foreword to *Selected Translations* he writes, "I began translating with the idea that it could teach me something about writing poetry. . . . It is love, I imagine, more than learning, that may eventually make it possible to be aware of the living resonance before it has words . . . and will impel one to be wary of any skill coming to shadow and doctor the source" (vii). Sheer love for the original makes him wary of altering or "doctoring" it. So as to preserve as much as possible the character of the original he keeps his translations extremely literal and faithful to the original. Perhaps partially because Merwin chooses to translate poems and prose poems informed by lightness, brilliance, or intimacy of tone, his translations often look and act like his own poems. He tends to translate poets who display his own ability to render the mysterious or the miraculous in the common and who can endow even the ordinary with a cosmic resonance. Still, paradoxically, his translations are literal equivalents of the originals, and he takes few liberties; but his spacing, his grouping of phrases and cadences, his line breaks, and his control of tone are all Merwin's own.

Although basically a blunter, earthier poet than Merwin, Roberto Juarroz writes a sublimely imaginative poetry which Merwin translates directly and honestly, infusing it with a slightly more ethereal quality than it has in the original:

> There will come a day
> when we won't need to push on the panes for them to fall,
> nor hammer the nails for them to hold,
> nor walk on the stones to keep them quiet,
> nor drink the faces of women for them to smile.
>
> It will be the beginning of the great union.
> Even God will learn how to talk,
> and the air and light
> will enter their cave of shy eternities.
> Then there'll be no more difference between your eyes and belly,
>
> between my words and my mouth.
> The stones will be like your breasts
> and I will make my verses with my hands
> so that nobody can be mistaken.[19]

Only a direct, forceful use of language and a light and airy tone could render this poem's lucidity. In fact, sometimes the question of influence—or more precisely the question of how deeply affected he may be by others' ways of creating poetry—is raised when a poem Merwin translates sounds as much like one of Merwin's own poems as Juarroz's "Sometimes My Hands Wake Me Up" (15) sounds like "Habits" (W, 28).

Merwin translates poems in verse and in prose. This intricately structured, richly textured poem by Neruda is an example of his prose translation:

Oh, each successive night that comes has something in it of an abandoned ember that is slowly burning out, and it falls swathed in ruins, surrounded by funereal objects. Ordinarily I am present at these ends, loaded with useless weapons, full of demolished objections. I preserve the clothing and the bones lightly impregnated with that semi-nocturnal substance: it is a temporal dust that in the end becomes a part of me, and the god of substitutions keeps watch at my side, breathing stubbornly, raising his sword.[20]

Possibly Merwin envisions a "god of substitutions" keeping watch over him as he translates, making sure that nothing essential to Neruda's poem—or any writer's—is lost.

The sensuous and sacred, earthy and reverential love poems in *Sanskrit Love Poetry* are a far cry from the luxuriant, rolling prose of Neruda, yet they reveal another dimension of Merwin's poetry, a love of life and sexuality. Here is part of a Sanskrit poem Merwin read at a recent poetry reading:

> to my mind her
> body unfurling
> with joy of being young
> flowering out of love
> her eyes floating as with wine and
> words wandering with love
> then the undoing of the knot
> of her sari
> that
> is Release[21]

Merwin produces two kinds of translations, one from the languages he knows—Spanish, French, German, Italian, and Latin—and another from languages he does not know. The first kind he translates entirely on his own. The other he translates through the intermediary of a native speaker or a fellow poet or scholar conversant in the language and literature of the country. This person gives him a literal English equivalent of the piece and counsels him on nuances, tone, and any special features or literary allusions in the poem. Naturally the Sanskrit and Russian translations are the outcome of the second kind of translation, and they add a new dimension to his literary corpus. A humor with no tinge of bitterness is a rarity in Merwin's work, yet it emanates from many of the Sanskrit poems. We are particularly fond of this one showing lovers gazing on mutual moons:

> The monk stares at
> her navel
> and she at the moon his face
> the crows steal
> both their
> spoon and their bowl[22]

This knowing and earthy humor recalls the humor and tone of Merwin's *Asian Figures*, a book of riddles and proverbs from all over Asia. He views these pithy axioms and traditional sayings as "fossil poetry" and in his Foreword offers some insight into what attracts him to the prose poem as well as to the new genre of the proverb: "There is an affinity which everyone must have noticed between poetry—certain kinds and moments of it—on the one hand, and such succinct forms as the proverb, the aphorism, the riddle, on the other. Poetry, on many occasions, gathers the latter under its name. But it seems to me likely that the proverb and its sisters are often poetry on their own, without the claim being made for them." The Foreword continues, giving the qualities that prose poems as well as proverbs share: "There are qualities that they obviously have in common: an urge to finality of utterance, for example, and to be irreducible and unchangeable" (AF, i).[23] The simplicity of diction in the prose resembles that of the proverb or aphorism; and each form can achieve a powerful impact by means of its finality of utterance, its mustering of authority in its tone and in its approach.

Jocularly, he goes on, "The urge to brevity is not perhaps as typical of poetry as we would sometimes wish, but the urge to be self-contained, to be whole, is perhaps another form of the same thing, and can be, and it is related to irreversibility in the words that is a mark of poetry." Another "blood-link" he notes is a concern with "the spoken idiom (my own, that is) [rather] than the written convention." This last blood-link is perhaps the signal characteristic of the prose and the proverb, both of which appear to have undergone a levelling of diction and style. They address the ordinary person and appeal to a shrewd, practical mentality rather than to emotion. Here is one of his proverbs: "Hard to hold out a cup farther than the heads of your children."

Clearly what tempts him to translate the proverb, riddle, or aphorism is not only its rootedness in natural fact, its analogical import and poetic value, but also its keen-edged traditional wisdom, honed into the briefest possible space. In all his poetry we note a general trend toward greater brevity and finality of utterance, a limpid simplicity. Merwin also displays a growing fascination with mythical thinking and a greater engagement with the material of the collective unconscious. Proverbs, riddles, and aphorisms appear to be a primal speech of mankind; they come unauthored and unsponsored into the world, and through translating them Merwin intends to make them fully enfranchised representatives of literary traditions, known parts of the literary heritage. Aphorisms, proverbs, and riddles are observations springing directly from the collective unconscious, now available to consciousness. They, like the anonymous medieval epics he translated at the beginning of his career, seem to be self-contained and whole because they are "sure tellings that do not start by justifying" (CL, 3).

A reading of Merwin's translations of *The Song of Roland* (1963) and his *The Poem of the Cid* (1959) would provide any student of epic poetry with a sure foundation in—and a substantial understanding of—the genre. Richard Howard claims that Merwin "has devised the finest versions I know of these great works, filtering out of the latter a narrative line of great importance to his own projects, 'a rough, spare, sinewy, rapid verse'; and in the former recognizing and recovering 'a clarity at once simple and formal, excited and cool, a certain limpidity not only in the language and the story but in the imagination behind them, qualities I find myself trying to describe in terms of light and water,'"[24] Here is the passage from *The Song of Roland* recounting Charlemagne's prophetic dream of the Battle of Roncesvalles: "Charles looks up toward heaven and sees thunderbolts, hail, rushing winds, storms and awesome tempests, and fires and flames appear to him, falling suddenly upon his whole army. The lances of ash wood and of apple wood catch fire and burn, and the shields, even to the gold bosses on them. . . . Then bears and leopards come to devour them, serpents and vipers, dragons and devils, and more than thirty thousand griffons.[25]

All Merwin's current translation and experimentation in unconventional poetic forms—epics, proverbs, aphorisms, fables, myths, and parables—enables him to travel through other poets' lands and consciousnesses and to inhabit their houses. His work in translation has always filled his need for renewal and refreshment by allowing him to speak in other voices and try out new poetic approaches. He identifies the motive of translation as "a wish to embrace, even through wrappings, poetry that was written from perspectives revealingly different from our own" (ST, vii). As he continues to translate, he also has recourse to a wide range of poetic forms, some traditional, some nontraditional, which afford him a means of experiencing other dimensions of reality.

VII   *The Transparence of the World and Word*

Amid all his literary forewords and notes on poetry, Merwin's Foreword to *Transparence of the World, Poems by Jean Follain* is a model of charm and lucidity. He clarifies Follain's steady, unchanging gaze for the reader about to embark on a journey through his poetry. Having given a few details of Follain's life, Merwin tells this anecdote illuminating Follain's view of language: "And when, in 1919, he was sent to England (Leeds) to learn the language, his resistance to the enterprise took the form of a refusal to believe that there was more than one way of naming a thing. The language, the words, in which he had learned to name particulars, were part of the uniqueness of the things named" (vii–viii). Follain's apprehension of language affirms the personality, humanity, and individuality of each separate word. He conceives of language as whole and primary—what we might mean by "first things first." In Merwin's work in translation and in his unconventional poetic forms as well as in Follain's poetry we are brought to primary terms of experience, confronting for the first time the actuality of the present. Our sense of contact with it derives from the freshness, the intimacy, and the nakedness of the revelations of the voice speaking. Merwin sees, along with Follain, Robert Creeley, and others, that all things are particular and reality itself is the specific content of an instant's possibility.[26] Merwin's poetry in prose or verse must be primary, bare, stripped of its nonessentials.

For Follain, his own language has a profound intimacy and integrity because of its strong bond with reality—words *are* things. His language has escaped the ravages of division after the linguistic dismemberment of Babel. The word's body has not been severed from the world's body;

the two are whole and intact, so that each element of the equation between world and word is transparent, a window into the other. Hence Merwin's title, *The Transparence of the World*.

Merwin's own ideals are primacy and a sense of the irreversibility of words in poetry. In writing a naked prose he attempts to restore the original transparency to language, and give it back its freshness. Certain words still stalking through our fables and stories retain their eternal meanings. In "A Voyage" he informs the reader that "*Wasa* . . . means the same thing, to start with, in every language, as soon as it is known" (H, 175). The profound and primal meaning of "Wasa" is the same in all languages: it is "water."

In "The Fragments" he crosses and recrosses the place of original union, becoming aware of "the fact that the event had never left the present. Parts of it keep appearing" (MP, 233). He sees remnants of it still around; but many are blocked from seeing them by minor differences in language, idiom, intonation, or tone which prevent one's seeing through to the source or seeing deeper meanings. Merwin's stance is always one of listening.

In a review of a book of poems, Stephen Spender explores the consciousness in all Merwin's poetry and prose:

> It is as though things write their own poems through Merwin. At their best, they are poems of total attention and as such they protest against our world of total distraction. He gives the reader the feeling that the things we see in nature can be withdrawn from our eyes and restored to their integral separateness; and that, in doing this, rituals and sacraments which have been lost and a sense of the sacredness of living are restored. He gives things the invisibility of covering darkness and then watches light re-create them for us.
>
> This is the poetry of the newness of every moment of creation. . . . Merwin has the capacity to make us see things which we feel we are aware of at the edge of consciousness. "These are days when the beetles hurry through dry grass hiding pieces of light they have stolen."[27]

Awareness at the edge of consciousness marks Merwin's work. And his manner of letting objects, places, and people relate their own stories in his imagination, seemingly at their dictation, is another of his poetic strengths: he can restore things "to their critical separateness." As he says at the end of "Unchopping a Tree," "Others are waiting. Everything is going to have to be put back" (MP, 88).

The atmosphere of expectancy runs strong in "The Unwritten"

where he imagines words crouching inside a pencil, waiting eagerly to be written:

> they're awake in there
> dark in the dark
> hearing us
> but they won't come out
> not for love not for time not for fire . . .
>
> what script can it be that they won't unroll
> in what language
> would I recognize it
> would I be able to follow it
> to make out the real names
> of everything
> maybe there aren't
> many
> it could be that there's only one word
> and it's all we need
> it's here in this pencil
>
> every pencil in the world
> is like this (W, 40)

The unwritten is the source of all his hope, all his will to write, and all his trepidations. Its potential makes him a poet of negative capability; he adheres to a negative aesthetic since what he awaits—"the real names of everything"—is not yet known, though it was known before and definitely will be again. He expressed his openness to the unknown in the negative when he said, "Everything that does not need you is real."

At present he is working at putting all the words on earth into their rightful "houses." He may know more about the inner life of words than anyone else. Certainly he has determined that "Some are like shrews, some are like birds, some are like water, or friends of various kinds, some are like old aunts, some are like lights, some are like feet walking without bodies in a hall lined with everything any of us remembers, . . ." (H, 43). He measures to each word its solitude and unique properties, specific density and origin, so that poetry, the work of the present and future, can supplant history with its counsel of despair. As much as the poet needs it, the unwritten needs him to translate, transcribe, or re-create it in a poem. Merwin looks toward the day of recognition when the necessary word or words are written by a common pencil and each person can say "farewell to his grief, to all that belongs to it, and go on without it, alone, complete, into the endless present" (MP, 95). At that point everything will be put back, "fragment after fragment."

CHAPTER 7

"Walking at Night Between the Two Deserts, Singing"

MERWIN'S personal life is a perpetual quest, a movement like that of Odysseus the conquering hero from "island to island, each with its entwining welcome, but none to call 'home.'" He realizes his true being in departure: in "The First Darkness," he writes, "Maybe he does not even have to exist / to exist in departures" (CL, 124). Merwin's poetry is a departure from fixed identity in that it delivers him from himself—" . . . my words are the garment of what I shall never be / Like the tucked sleeve of a one-armed boy."

Why should he return to a conventional life? Merwin's poetry and prose on family life are devastating images of individual hells. His "Uncle Hess" in *The Drunk in the Furnace*, "Letter Home" in *The Moving Target*, and "Aunt Mary" published in *Antaeus* in 1976 (but not in *Houses and Travellers*) vividly reveal the "No Exit" situations from which Noah's raven, "the son of stars never seen," has exited. Because no settled life can contain or content him, Merwin persists in a nomadic way of life. The journey is one of the major motifs in his work. Of complementary interest is the motif of discovery: his poems occasionally tell of the one real key or the single secret of the world. One poem is significantly titled "Speakers of the Word for Heaven": the name refers to the concept of the original symbolic language he and Emerson share. He adheres to the ideal of a fundamental apocalyptic reduction of the universe through the unfastening power of the word. Latent in many of his poems is the implication that total knowledge is intuitive, spontaneous, and can only be discovered all at once: to speak the correct word for heaven might effect the establishment of a heaven on earth.

Merwin finds travel both necessary financially and stimulating aesthetically. Instead of staying in one spot and "getting nowhere but older," he decamps, wearing out his only shoes and advising, "Look at

159

their shoes / to see how gravely / they are hurt" (CL, 118). His spirit is always young, whatever the condition of his shoes.

He has indeed throughout his thirty-year career "studied one song." Sometimes his poetry and prose have generated myths, but more often he has himself embodied one to perfection, hence his widespread popularity among college audiences. His great appeal derives from the fact that in a heroless decade he *is* a kind of folk hero: he refused to sign the loyalty oath to the state of New York at Buffalo, and upon receiving the Pulitzer Prize he gave the prize money to a painter blinded by police fire in the Berkeley riots. In each instance, integrity necessitated the stand he took; he is a person of physical courage in a time when personal, physical, and moral bravery go largely unremarked.

Personally he combines the charm and grace of an Old World gentleman with the virtues of wit, humor, courage, loyalty, discretion, and ingenuity. His character proves that the chivalric hero was always at least partially *puer aeternis*. If Merwin's "one song" grows monotonous in *The Compass Flower,* that may be because in choosing not to choose he has indeed chosen. He may have resisted entering space and time completely, but still his life takes a definite, even predictable course. Those who charge that his work is vague and distant cannot deny that "our voices in their heads waken / childhoods in other tongues." There is a constant freshness and spontaneity in his poetic voice, an intelligence in his prose, and an intimacy in all his work which is the seal and standard of W. S. Merwin.

I   *New Wine in New Bottles*

In the final analysis, Merwin's recent poetry may not be monotonous or weak at all; it may not be attaining to the condition of silence; it may be misjudged. In actuality, some of the poems of *The Compass Flower* and the recent prose pieces may manifest a radical departure in the evolution of Merwin's writing. They may manifest a new literary perspective, even a new genre.

The Moving Target signalled Merwin's last radical break with tradition in poetry. Several poems in that book anticipated the surprise of critics encountering his "new style" for the first time. One poem, whimsically titled "Air," speaks of the "strange sound" his poetry makes and of his need to go "my way":

> Naturally it is night.
> Under the overturned lute with its

> One string I am going my way
> Which has a strange sound. (MT, 50)

Recent critical reactions to *The Compass Flower* fulfilled the prediction implicit in these lines by remarking that the book has a strange sound. It is mysterious, "night," to the critics since Merwin's poetic departures, which seem to occur every fifteen years, are crossings of the "desert of the unknown, / Big enough for my feet" (MT, 10). "Air" ends:

> This must be what I wanted to be doing,
> Walking at night between the two deserts,
> Singing. (MT, 50)

Understanding the transformations in Merwin's poetry demands imaginative leaps that some critics, even the most accomplished, find it difficult to make. Following him into aesthetic dimensions "Big enough for my feet" can tax the wits and overturn all one's expectations of a work of art. With Emerson, Merwin believes that "Consistency is the hobgoblin of little minds." He conceives of the bemused, benighted critics as "old bottles": "Snug on the crumbling earth,/ The old bottles lay dreaming of new wine" (MT, 30). They may *dream* of new wine, he suggests, but they may not recognize it upon waking.

New wine is exactly what Merwin has prepared for his readers in his recent work, new wine in *new* bottles. Though this wine may appear to have been poured into the old bottles of traditional poetic form, in fact it was not. Merwin's movement through prose, proselike poems, and translation has been a search for new bottles, new vessels to contain aesthetic impetus. In a desire to view life from other dimensions, he effects a genre shift in the recent prose and some of the poetry. What appears on the page may retain the *look* of a poem or prose poem, but the work has merged aesthetically with a genre that is traditionally considered the dynamic source of art rather than a genre in its own right—myth. If one conceives of the raw verbal art of parabolic, dreamlike storytelling as having purposes markedly different from the purposes of a novel, say, or a short story or a poem, then one can conceive of the evolving literary genre of myth. Operating generically, myth renders scenes and characters in literal situations redolent of the universal. The emphasis is on declarative, direct expression of meaning rather than on linguistic complexity. A surface simplicity typifies this genre, and the simplicity is a simplicity of refreshment and renewal, not a crude or mindless simplicity. It is as though Merwin and his writing had passed through the point of disappearance mentioned in "The Dwelling" and ceased to move in a known and visible aesthetic dimension. The poet has ceased to exist; the storyteller/mythmaker is born and speaks from these analeptic lines.

In an article called "Language and Myth," Albert Cook speaks of poetry's plunging into myth as a strategy of renewal any writer can avail himself of, a "strategy for returning the poetic performance in language to the power lying in the source of poetry, in myth."[1] Returning to the source and speaking from that source are Merwin's goals in the newest work.

Paul Ricoeur characterizes the mythic dimension as that level of literary experience where language's "function of discovery is set free."[2] Poems and prose poems become narratives in quest of other dimensions of literary discourse. They dream of new bottles for new wine; they are metaphors for and distillations of universal human experience. Some poems of *The Compass Flower* and many of the prose poems fall into the genre of myth. Though Merwin may still consider what he is producing poetry, actually he, Snyder, Bly, and others are quietly crafting a new genre in certain of their recent works.

As a genre, myth embraces all unselfconscious tellings, from the primitive shaman's stories to the more highly wrought prose poems, poetry, and texts of these major contemporary figures. In myth, the focus is on narrative, on the telling of a story, rather than on characterization. The lyrical movement is a movement in archetypes and in rhythmic, expressive language. Skillful manipulation of language or technical artistry are not permitted to usurp the aesthetic interest. Instead the interest in each work arises from a juxtaposition of events and human action so as to create a flowing narrative in which the sequence of events takes precedence over the teller or any individual in the tale. A tone of wonder animates the whole. Increased reliance on a narrative that generates universality, the use of generic language, and an earthy curiosity—all these are habitual characteristics of myth and of Merwin's recent work.

Short-circuiting the usual process whereby myth informs literature that already possesses its own genre, here Merwin draws directly on the animating force of myth. Pouring the new wine of his dramatic stories into the new bottles of the genre of myth, he fuses story to poem until the work becomes a unique creation. He expands his scope freely and heuristically, charting a "desert of the unknown," a genre with roots in the oldest source of literature. Other contemporary writers have discovered and even landed on this terrain, too, but no critic has as yet explored it. Conceiving of myth as a genre *may* be a way of encompassing and finding a generic homeland for many of the new works of Robert Bly, Gary Snyder, Russell Edson, Michael Benedikt as well as Merwin.

The question arises, how is this engagement with myth different from Merwin's original employment of myth in his first four books of poems? At the outset, Merwin writes as the devoted student of Graeco-Roman and Hebrew myth, the great texts of Western culture. He successively embodies these myths in poetry as if to prove his worthiness of the title of poet and to establish his reputation as master of the craft of verse. He writes in "Learning a Dead Language," "What you remember becomes yourself / . . . What you remember saves you" (F, 176–77) so he remembers in order to be saved. And he tries unsuccessfully to "become" what he beholds and embodies. Just as Yeats tried on and wore his "coat of old mythologies," Merwin tries on myth after myth. From Proteus to the Prodigal Son, he experiments, assuming various new mythic identities and finally discarding them all as Yeats cast off his coat.

In the recent work, however, Merwin himself is the source of myth. He does not need to learn or remember the myths that inform his writing since he is the mythmaker. Like the parables of Kafka, Merwin's poem/myths resemble circles whose centers are everywhere and whose circumferences are nowhere. Difficult to limit to any one frame of reference, these vital myths are filled with concrete objects, experiences, and events redolent of the mystery that makes life. Probing ontological questions, they touch deeper grounds of being than the crafted, highly wrought early poetry.

In a sense Merwin has come, in the course of his career, full circle from one engagement with myth to another, but that circle twists in an upward spiral, describing the winding of a gyre. His recent work is not a return to but the final expulsion of the inherited corpus of "old mythologies." Merwin now generates his own myths, as he generates his own identity. Having cast off the remembered myths of Western civilization, he is free to savor his own mythic ideas. Readers who valued the trenchant wit and poignant ironies of *The Lice* may be disappointed to find no Book of Kings, no prophets in *The Compass Flower*, a book that intuitively takes the flower as its compass. The poet they thought they knew has abandoned his style of poetry and dropped out of sight, disappearing into the unknown dwelling of myth. Perhaps myth is the accompaniment that was still unfinished in 1973 with the publication of *Writings to an Unfinished Accompaniment.*

In *The Rule of Metaphor* Paul Ricoeur states that "To interpret a work is to display the world to which it refers by virtue of its 'arrangement,' its 'genre,' and its 'style.'"[3] The fact that W. S. Merwin is in the process of shifting genres and constructing a new dwelling, a new arrangement and style for the genre, makes it imperative to invoke a new set of critical standards for judging his work. To evaluate his recent work on the basis of what has come before is fruitless. Each poem/myth must be considered anew as manifesting a different genre since, as Ricoeur says, those who have not recognized the world to which the writer refers cannot adequately display it and are unqualified to interpret it. Not recognizing that Merwin's new "singing" is effecting a genre shift into myth has left a lot of critics, myself included, in the dark. "Naturally it is night."

Notes and References

Chapter One

1. (Chicago 1969), p. 24.
2. "A Reading of Galway Kinnell," *Iowa Review* 1 (Winter 1970): 66–67.
3. "In a Dark Time," *The Collected Poems of Theodore Roethke* (Garden City, N.Y., 1975), p. 231.
4. *The Situation of Poetry* (Princeton, 1976), p. 94.
5. "The term [Deep Image] refers to a concrete particular that has attracted and operates in a context of powerful feelings and associations in the unconscious of the reader when it appears in an imaginatively conceived and ordered poem. The deep image carries the original affective power of a pattern of new and even surprising verbal combinations, contributing their force. As Kelly puts it, 'Poetry, like dream reality, is the juncture of the experienced with the never experienced, it is the fulfillment of the imagined and the unimagined.'" Stephan Stepanchev, *American Poetry Since 1945* (New York, 1965), p. 177.
6. *The Situation of Poetry* pp. 164–65.
7. The inspiration for the foregoing material on "The Drunk in the Furnace" was provided by "Speaking from Within the Furnace," an unpublished paper by Gary Thompson of California State University, Chico. Mr. Thompson wrote the paper while taking a graduate seminar in Contemporary Poetry at the University of Montana and presented it on June 1, 1973.
8. *The Situation of Poetry*, p. 165.
9. Both of the above quotations are by Sandra McPherson, "Saying No: A Brief Compendium and Sometimes a Workbook with Blank Spaces," *Iowa Review* 4 (Summer 1973): 84.
10. *New World Writing 12* (New York, 1957), p. 154.
11. When I speak of the Biblical myths in Merwin's poetry, I am subscribing to the definition of myth set down by Robert Graves: "Myths are dramatic stories that form a sacred charter either authorizing the continuance of ancient institutions, customs, rites, and beliefs . . . or approving alterations." *Hebrew Myths* (Garden City, N.Y., 1974), p. 11.
12. Letter to the author, dated December 3, 1974.
13. (New York, 1969), p. viii.
14. *Alone with America* (New York, 1969), p. 355.
15. (New Haven, 1952), p. vii.
16. "Myth in the Poetry of W. S. Merwin," *Poets in Progress*, ed. Edward Hungerford (Evanston, Ill., 1962), p. 186.

17. Ibid., p. 182.

18. Ibid., pp. 180–81.

19. Hugh Kenner, *The Pound Era* (Berkeley, 1971), p. 39.

20. *Alone with America*, p. 354.

21. Ibid.

22. W. S. Merwin, "To Name the Wrong," *The Nation* 194 (February 24, 1962): 176.

23. *Mythologies (New York, 1972), p. 69.*

24. *Opus Posthumous* (New York, 1957), p. 239.

25. *Voices*, p. 27.

26. (New York, 1965), p. 130.

27. *Collected Poems* (New York, 1961), pp 496–97.

28. *Palm at the End of the Mind* (New York, 1971), p. 397. This poem does not appear in Stevens's *Collected Poems*.

29. *Collected Poems*, p. 382.

30. Ibid., p. 167.

31. Ibid., p. 177

32. *Selected Prose of Robert Frost*, ed., Hyde Cox and Edward Connery Lathem (New York, 1966), p. 44.

Chapter Two

1. "An American Primer," in *Walt Whitman, A Critical Anthology*, ed. A. Francis Murphy (Baltimore, 1970), pp. 70–72.

2. *The Double Agent* (Gloucester, Mass., 1962), p. 81.

3. "The Animals," *One Foot in Eden* (New York, 1956), p. 16.

4. "A Poet in Exile," *New York Review of Books*, March 17, 1966, p 18.

5. Letter to Paul Carroll, November 16, 1967, quoted in Carroll's *The Poem in its Skin* (Chicago, 1968), p. 150.

6. Merwin defines "diction" in his essay on French Classical Theatre thus: "I use the word diction to include everything organized and everything of the organization from the sounds of the words to the patterned actions of the speakers" (Quoted in Richard Howard's *Alone with America*, p. 356).

7. Quoted in "A Poet in Exile," p. 18.

8. *The Poem in its Skin*, p. 150.

9. (New York, 1976), p. 474.

Chapter Three

1. Richard Howard in *Alone With America*, p. 356.

2. Ibid., p. 371.

3. *Poets in Progress* (Evanston, 1962), p. 185.

4. *Crowell's Handbook of Contemporary American Poetry* (New York, 1973), p. 213.

5. Dust jacket of *Some Spanish Ballads*, trans. W. S. Merwin, (London, 1961).

6. *Alone With America*, p. 365.

7. Ibid., p. 356.

8. *The Poem in its Skin*, p. 150n.

9. *Alone With America*, p. 352.

10. "Speaking from Within the Furnace," p. 3.

11. *Crowell's Handbook*, p. 213

12. "Crunk," [pseud.] "The Work of W. S. Merwin," *The Sixties*, No. 4 (Fall, 1960), p. 35.

13. "Speaking from Within the Furnace," p. 3.

14. *Alone With America*, pp. 370–71.

15. "Speaking from Within the Furnace," p. 4.

16. *Alone With America*, p. 371.

17. All quotations in this paragraph from "Speaking from Within the Furnace," p. 4.

Chapter Four

1. Anthony Libby, "W. S. Merwin and the Nothing That Is," *Contemporary Literature* 16 (Winter 1975): 29–30.

2. *Alone with America*, p. 364.

3. "Speaking from Within the Furnace," p. 4.

4. *The Collected Poems of W. B. Yeats* (New York: The Macmillan Co., 1968), p. 125.

5. *Alone with America*, p. 372.

6. Ibid., p. 374.

7. See "Some Questions of Precision," *Poetry* 101 (June 1964): 184–5.

8. Quoted in *Alone with America*, p. 375.

9. Ibid, p. 373

10. Ibid., p. 372.

11. *Crowell's Handbook*, p. 213.

12. Quoted in *Alone with America*, p. 353.

13. "The Loss That Has Not Left This Place: The Problem of Form in the Poetry of W. S. Merwin," Unpublished Dissertation University of Iowa, (1975), p. 12.

14. "The Continuities of W. S. Merwin," *Massachusetts Review* 14 (Summer 1973): 572.

15. "The Loss That Has Not Left This Place," p. 12.

16. Ibid.

17. The phrase "these disstated things" occurs later in "Cancion y glosa," (*F*, 48).

18. *Alone with America*, p. 357.

19. "W. S. Merwin: A Critical Accompaniment," *Boundary 2* 4 (Fall 1975): 190.

20. Ibid.

21. All quotations in this passage are from the dissertation abstract of Mary Slowik, "The Loss That Has Not Left This Place: The Problem of Form in the Poetry of W. S. Merwin," *DAI* 36 (1976), 8064A.

22. "Speaking from Within the Furnace," p. 4.

23. "A Riddle for the New Year: Affirmation in W. S. Merwin," *Modern Poetry Studies* 4 (Winter 1973): 294.

24. *Massachusetts Review*, 14: 572.

25. Ibid., p. 585.

26. *Voices*, p. 31.

27. "Notes for a Preface," *The Distinctive Voice*, ed. William J. Martz (Glenview, Ill., 1966), p. 269.

28. Ibid., all quotations in this passage are from p. 272.

Chapter Five

1. Octavio Paz, *The Bow and the Lyre* (Austin, 1973), p. 98.

2. "Writing for the End," *New York Review of Books*, May 6, 1971, p. 27.

3. *Modern Poetry Studies* 5 (1974); 87–91.

4. "The Art of Poetry," *Paris Review* 15 (Winter 1977): 76.

5. Denis Donoghue, "Objects Solitary and Terrible," *New York Review of Books*, June 6, 1968, p. 23.

6. *The Distinctive Voice*, p. 269.

7. Ibid.

8. "The Poet," *The Complete Works of Ralph Waldo Emerson*, Centinary Edition, III (Boston, 1903), p. 21.

9. *The Distinctive Voice*, p. 272.

10. "The Loss That Has Not Left This Place," p. 238.

11. "Language Against Itself" in *American Poetry Since 1960, Some Critical Perspectives*, ed. Robert Shaw (London, 1973) p. 65.

12. *New York Review of Books*, May 6, 1971,p. 20.

13. "The Loss That Has Not Left This Place," p. 256.

14. Ibid., p. 236.

15. *Boundary 2* 4 (Fall 1975): 192.

16. "A Poetry of Darkness," *Nation* 211 (December 14, 1970): 634.

17. Irving Massey, *The Uncreating Word* (Bloomington, Ind., 1970), p. 88.

18. *Boundary 2* 4 (Fall 1975): 195.

19. *New York Review of Books*, June 6, 1968, p. 22.

20. *Contemporary Authors* 13–16, ed. James M. Etheridge and Barbara Kopala (Detroit, 1966), p. 299.

21. "Speaking from Within the Furnace," p. 6.

22. "Introduction," *American Poetry Since 1960*, p. 3.

23. "The Loss That Has Not Left This Place," p. 256.

24. *Crowell's Handbook*, pp. 214–15.

25. For more insights into the role of time in Merwin's poetry, see Cheri Davis, "Time and Timelessness in the Poetry of W. S. Merwin," *Modern Poetry Studies* 6 (Winter 1975): 224–36.

26. "Speaking from Within the Furnace," p. 6.

27. "The Loss That Has Not Left This Place," pp. 2–3.

28. Quoted in Laurette Veza, "La Poésie de W. S. Merwin: Silence Notre Premier Langage," *Études Anglaises* 29 (1976): 521.

29. *Selected Essays* (New York, 1954), p. 180.

30. Thomas R. Whitaker, *William Carlos Williams* (New York, 1968), p. 19.

31. Introductory editorial comment to the selections by Merwin in *The Norton Anthology of Modern Poetry*, ed., Richard Ellmann and Robert O'Clair (New York, 1973), p. 1168.

32. "The Loss That Has Not Left This Place," p. 10.

33. *Modern Poetry Studies* 4: 294.

34. "At the Poles of Poetry," *New York Review of Books*, August 17, 1978, p. 48.

35. *New York Times Book Review*, June 19, 1977, pp. 15, 37.

36. "Speaking from Within the Furnace," p. 6.

37. *Transparence of the World, Poems by Jean Follain*, selected and translated by W. S. Merwin (New York, 1969), p. 81. For more information on the literary relationship between Merwin and Follian, see the unpublished doctoral dissertation by Cheri Davis, "Radical Innocence: A Thematic Study of the Relationship between the Translator and the Translated in the Poetry of W. S. Merwin and Jean Follain," University of Southern California, 1973.

38. *The Distinctive Voice*, pp. 269–72.

39. *Complete Works*, Centinary Edition, III, 8.

40. *Ralph Waldo Emerson*, UMPAW 41 (1964), pp. 40–42.

41. *Complete Works*, Centinary Edition, III, 18.

42. *The Distinctive Voice*, p. 271.

43. *The Collected Works of Ralph Waldo Emerson*, ed. Alfred R. Ferguson (Cambridge, Mass., 1971), I, 21.

44. Fortunately, since the publication of this poem in 1967, the gray whale population has enjoyed a resurgence.

Chapter Six

1. "Diminishing Returns: The Writings of W. S. Merwin," in *American Poetry Since 1960*, p. 80.

2. *New York Review of Books*, June 6, 1968, p. 23.

3. (New York, 1976), p. 47.

4. Robert Bly, "Mixed Parables," *New York Times Book Review*, February 5, 1978, p. 14.

5. *The Prose Poem*, pp. 48–49.

6. "A Poetry of Darkness," p. 634.

7. *Transparence of the World*, p. vi.

8. David Ossman, *The Sullen Art* (New York, 1963), pp. 66–67.

9. "The Dwelling of Disappearance: W. S. Merwin's *The Lice*," *Modern Poetry Studies* 3 (1972): 119, 121.

10. Ibid., p. 121.

11. Ibid., p. 124.

12. Ibid., p. 123–4.

13. Ibid., p. 128.

14. Quoted in Thomas Whitaker, *William Carlos Williams*, p. 19.

15. *The Duino Elegies*, trans. David Young (New York, 1978), p. 19.

16. *American Poetry Since 1960*, p. 80.

17. "On Being Awarded the Pulitzer Prize," *New York Review of Books*, June 3, 1971, p. 41.

18. "Comment," *Poetry* 115 (December, 1969): 187–89.

19. Roberto Juarroz, *Vertical Poetry*, trans. W. S. Merwin (Santa Cruz, Cal., 1977) p. 23.

20. Pablo Neruda, *Selected Poems*, ed. Nathaniel Tarn (New York, 1972), p. 71.

21. *Sanskrit Love Poetry*, trans. W. S. Merwin and J. Moussaieff Masson (New York, 1977), p. 167.

22. Ibid., p. 41.

23. *Asian Figures*, trans. W. S. Merwin (New York, 1973).

24. *Alone with America*, p. 352.

25. *The Song of Roland*, trans. W. S. Merwin (New York, 1963) p. 70.

26. See Robert Creeley, *A Quick Graph* (San Francisco, 1970), p. 68.

27. "Can Poetry Be Reviewed?", *New York Review of Books*, September 20, 1973, p. 11.

Chapter Seven

1. *Boundary 2* 5 (Spring 1977): 662.

2. *The Rule of Metaphor*, trans. Robert Czerny (Toronto, 1977), p. 247.

3. Ibid., p. 220.

Selected Bibliography

PRIMARY SOURCES

Poetry and Prose
Animae. San Francisco: Kayak Press, 1969.
Asian Figures. New York: Atheneum, 1973.
The Carrier of Ladders. New York: Atheneum, 1970.
The Compass Flower. New York: Atheneum, 1977.
The Dancing Bears. New Haven: Yale University Press, 1954.
The Drunk in the Furnace. New York: The Macmillan Company, 1960.
The First Four Books of Poems. New York: Atheneum, 1975. Contains *A Mask for Janus, The Dancing Bears, Green with Beasts,* and *The Drunk in the Furnace.*
Green with Beasts. New York: A. A. Knopf, 1956.
Houses and Travellers. New York: Atheneum, 1977.
The Lice. New York: Atheneum, 1967.
A Mask for Janus. New Haven: Yale University Press, 1952.
The Miner's Pale Children. New York: Atheneum, 1970.
The Moving Target. New York: Atheneum, 1963
A New Right Arm. Albuquerque: Road Runner Press, 1970.
Signs. Iowa City: Stone Walls Press, 1970.
Writings to an Unfinished Accompaniment. New York: Atheneum, 1973.

Play
"Favor Island." *New World Writing 12.* New York: New American Library, 1957.

Translations
Euripides: Iphigeneia at Aulis. Trans. with George E. Dimock, Jr. New York: Oxford University Press, 1978.
The Life of Lazarillo de Tormes: His Fortunes and Adversities. New York: Doubleday & Co., 1962.
Osip Mandelstam: Selected Poems. Trans. with Clarence Brown. New York: Atheneum, 1974.
The Poem of the Cid. New York: New American Library, 1959.
Products of the Perfected Civilization: Selected Writings of Chamfort. New York: The Macmillan Co., 1969.
Sanskrit Love Poetry. Trans. with J. Moussaieff Masson. New York: Columbia University Press, 1977.

171

The Satires of Persius. Bloomington: Indiana University Press, 1961.
Selected Translations 1948-1968. New York: Atheneum, 1969.
Selected Translations 1968-1978. New York: Atheneum, 1979.
Some Spanish Ballads. London: Abelard-Schuman, 1961.
The Song of Roland. New York: Vintage, 1963.
Transparence of the World, Poems by Jean Follain. New York: Atheneum, 1969.
Twenty Poems of Love and a Song of Despair. Poems by Pablo Neruda. London: Cape Editions, 1969.
Vertical Poetry. Poems by Roberto Juarroz. Santa Cruz, California: Kayak, 1977.

Commentary on Poetry and the Poet's Role
Foreword to *Asian Figures*. New York: Atheneum, 1973. Pp. ii–iii.
Foreword to *Selected Translations 1948-1968*. New York: Atheneum, 1969. Pp. vii–ix.
Foreword to *Selected Translations 1968-1978*. New York: Atheneum, 1979. Pp. vii–xiv.
Foreword to *Transparence of the World, Poems by Jean Follain*. New York: Atheneum, 1969. Pp. iv–viii.
Introduction to *Voices*, Aphorisms by Antonio Porchia. Chicago: Big Table, 1969. N. p.
Notes for a Preface, in *The Distinctive Voice*. Edited by William J. Martz. Glenview, Ill.: Scott, Foresman and Co., 1966. Pp. 268–72.
"On Being Awarded the Pulitzer Prize." *New York Review of Books*, June 3, 1971, p. 41.
"On Open Form," in *The New Naked Poetry*. Edited by Stephen Berg and Robert Mezey. Indianapolis: Bobbs-Merrill, 1976. Pp. 276–78.
"A Poet in Exile." Review of Edwin Muir's *Collected Poems*. *New York Review of Books*, March 17, 1966, pp. 16–18.
"To Name the Wrong." *The Nation* 194 (February 24, 1962): 176.
"W. S. Merwin," in *The Sullen Art*. Edited by David Ossman. New York: Corinth, 1963. Pp. 65–72. Interview with Ossman.

SECONDARY SOURCES

Parts of Books and Articles
ATLAS, JAMES. "Diminishing Returns: The Writings of W. S. Merwin."In *American Poetry Since 1960, Some Critical Perspectives*. Ed. Robert B. Shaw. London: Carcanet, 1974, pp. 69–81. In a well-written, dour, trenchant analysis of Merwin's poetry of the early 1970s, Atlas compares Merwin with Williams and the poet of the Objectivist school and finds Merwin wanting.
BENSTON, ALICE, "Myth in the Poetry of W. S. Merwin." In *Poets in Progress*. Ed. Edward Hungerford. Evanston: Northwestern University Press,

1962, pp. 179–204. In a valuable early essay, Benston focuses on the role of myth in Merwin's first three books of poems.

BLY, ROBERT. "Mixed Parables" [Review of *Houses and Travellers*]. *New York Times Book Review*, February 5, 1978, pp. 14–15. At the outset Bly takes a judicious approach to Merwin's prose pieces, but he finishes by saying that the book should have been cut substantially. The twenty-year rivalry between Merwin and Bly, carried on mainly by Bly, parades itself, thinly disguised, in this review.

———. "The Work of W. S. Merwin." *The Sixties* No. 4 (Fall 1960): 32–43. Bly, alias Crunk, assails Merwin's poetry for vagueness, lack of poetic intensity and vitality, colorlessness. He concedes, however, that several poems in *The Drunk in the Furnace* are very good.

CARROLL, PAUL. "The Spirit with Long Ears and Paws." Chapter on "Lemuel's Blessing." In *The Poem in its Skin*. Chicago: Big Table, 1968, pp. 139–52. In a thorough, insightful analysis of Merwin's psalmic poem "Lemuel's Blessing," Carroll explores wilderness and dream animal imagery as well as Merwin's philosophy of poetic composition.

CARRUTH, HAYDEN. "*The Compass Flower* by W. S. Merwin." *New York Times Book Review*, June 19, 1977, pp. 15, 37. Because he has long been an ardent admirer of Merwin's work, Carruth regrets the diminishment in verbal power and the vagueness he witnesses in *The Compass Flower*.

DAVIS, CHERYL C. "Merwin's Odysseus." *Concerning Poetry* 8 (Spring 1975): 25–33. Taking the poem "Odysseus" as the point of departure, the article traces the development of Merwin's concept of the treacherous fallibility of memory from the period of *The Drunk in the Furnace* through that of *The Miner's Pale Children*.

———. "Time and Timelessness in the Poetry of W. S. Merwin." *Modern Poetry Studies* 6 (1975): 224–36. The author examines the polarity of time and timelessness in Merwin's poetry through *The Carrier of Ladders*.

DICKEY, JAMES. "W. S. Merwin." In *Babel to Byzantium*. New York: Octagon, 1973, pp 142–3. This critical piece, written in the early 1960s, is qualifiedly favorable, though it states that Merwin lacks "some vital ingress into the event of the poem."

DONOGHUE, DENIS. "Objects Solitary and Terrible" [Review of *The Lice*]. *New York Review of Books*, June 6, 1968, pp. 22–23. A highly perceptive, sensitively conceived review of *The Lice*, perhaps the best review of this book published.

———. "Writing for the End" [Review of *The Carrier of Ladders*]. *New York Review of Books* 16 May 6, 1971: 27–28. In an excellent review, Donoghue treats Merwin's sense of an ending and his poetic movement into the void.

DORN, EDWARD. "Some Questions of Precision" [Review of *The Moving Target*]. *Poetry* 101 (1964): 184–85. In this acidic review, Dorn says he prefers Merwin's early poetic style or even his prose style in *A New Right Arm* to the new Surrealistic style of *The Moving Target*.

ETHERIDGE, JAMES M. and BARBARA KOPALA, eds "W. S. Merwin." In *Contemporary Authors*, xiii–xvi. Detroit: Gale Research, 1966, pp. 299–300. The only published information on Merwin's childhood and youth, this account of his personal and poetic origins contains a fascinating early comment on how he began writing poetry.

GORDON, JAN B. "The Dwelling of Disappearance: W. S. Merwin's *The Lice*." *Modern Poetry Studies* 3 (1972): 119–38. Gordon investigates "the dwelling of disappearance" in *The Lice* and *The Miner's Pale Children*. This is one of the most perceptive, penetrating articles linking Merwin's prose poems with *The Lice*.

HOWARD, RICHARD. "A Poetry of Darkness" [Review of *The Carrier of Ladders* and *The Miner's Pale Children*]. *Nation* 211 (December 14,1970): 634–5. This excellent review by the dean of Merwin scholarship sheds light on similar themes, images, and approaches in the books of poetry and prose.

———. "We Survived the Selves That We Remembered." In *Alone with America*. New York: Atheneum, 1969, pp. 349–80. This remains the finest single work of criticism on the poetic corpus of W. S. Merwin. Howard's brilliant assessment of Merwin's career through the publication of *The Lice* is soon to be revised to encompass the poetry and prose published since then.

KYLE, CAROL. "A Riddle for the New Year: Affirmation in W. S. Merwin." *Modern Poetry Studies* 4 (1973): 288–303. This article skillfully traces the riddle of the new year, the motif of beginning, and the growing affirmation implicit in Merwin's poetry.

LEVINE, PHILIP. "Comment" [Review of *Selected Translations 1948–1968*]. *Poetry* 115 (1969): 187–89. Levine's light, favorable review is the predecessor of a number of more exhaustive doctoral studies of Merwin's translations.

LEIBERMAN, LAURENCE. "The Church of Ash." In *Unassigned Frequencies, American Poetry in Review, 1964–1977*. Urbana: University of Illinois Press, 1977, pp. 122–32. In a review of *Writings to an Unfinished Accompaniment* Leiberman analyzes "Merwin's scrupulous negativity [which] is the fiercest poetic discipline around."

LIBBY, ANTHONY. "W. S. Merwin and the Nothing That Is." *Contemporary Literature* 16 (1975): 19–40. Highly philosophical and astute, Libby's article is one of the best treating Merwin's negative aesthetic.

MACSHANE, FRANK. "A Portrait of W. S. Merwin." *Shenandoah* 21, ii (1970): 3–14. Here MacShane works toward an assessment of Merwin's aesthetic theories and his ideas about his own writing.

MALKOFF, KARL. "W. S. Merwin." In *Crowell's Handbook of Contemporary American Poetry*. New York: Thomas Y. Crowell, 1973, pp. 208–17. In an essay tracing the evolution of Merwin's poetry up through *The Carrier of Ladders*, Malkoff provides a clear introductory summary of Merwin's poetic career and aims.

MCPHERSON, SANDRA. "Saying No: A Brief Compendium and Sometimes a Workbook with Blank Spaces." *The Iowa Review* 4 (1973): 84–88. A sketchy, "journalit" treatment of Merwin's—and other poets'—negative aesthetic.

RAMSEY, JAROLD. "The Continuities of W. S. Merwin." *Massachusetts Review* 14 (1973): 572–98. This article, containing an intriguing discussion of apocalyptic preoccupations in *The Lice*, shows the underlying continuity of Merwin's complete *oeuvre*.

SPENDER, STEPHEN. "Can Poetry Be Reviewed?" *New York Review of Books*, September 20, 1973, pp. 8–14. Spender seems to be speaking of Merwin's outlook in all his poetry when he writes of the watchful, receptive stance of *Writings to an Unfinished Accompaniment*.

VEZA, LAURETTE. "La Poésie de W. S. Merwin: Silence Notre Premier Langage." *Études Anglaises* 29 (1976): 510–21. The only treatment of the role of silence in Merwin's poetry, Veza's article is not wholly accurate.

ZUCKER, DAVID H. "In Search of the Simplicities" [Review of *Writings to an Unfinished Accompaniment* and *Asian Figures*]. *Modern Poetry Studies* 5 (1974): 87–91. This short, succinct review is expecially valuable for those interested in *Asian Figures*.

Dissertations and Unpublished Papers

DAVIS, CHERI C. "Radical Innocence: A Thematic Study of the Relationship between the Translator and the Translated in the Poetry of W. S. Merwin and Jean Follain." Dissertation, University of Southern California, 1973. This is the first study of the polarity between the translator and the translated in Merwin's poetry and Follain's poetry. The focus is on *Transparence of the World* and its thematic and phenomenological relevance to Merwin's own poetry.

SLOWIK, MARY. "The Loss That Has Not Left This Place: The Problem of Form in the Poetry of W. S. Merwin." Dissertation, University of Iowa, 1975. This is the best dissertation I have encountered on Merwin's corpus, though regrettably it only covers the poetry up to *The Carrier of Ladders*. Especially good on the problem of form in *The Lice*.

THOMPSON, GARY. "Speaking from Within the Furnace." Unpublished Paper written for a Graduate Seminar at the University of Montana, June 1, 1973. Keen insights into the inner and outer functions of silence in Merwin's poetry.

THOMPSON, RUTH FOSNESS. "The Quest for Harmony: A Thematic Analysis of the Poetry of W. S. Merwin." Dissertation, University of Minnesota, 1977. Quite an intelligent, thorough thematic study of Merwin's poetic evolution and his overriding quest for harmony.

Index